Life's Curves and Crossroads:

My Story

Mark Irabor

Scripture taken from the King James Version KJV). Copyright © 2017 by Thomas Nelson Publishing. Used by permission.

ISBN: 979-8-9897932-0-4 (Paperback)
ISBN: 979-8-9897932-1-1 (E-book – EPUB)

Library of Congress Control Number: 2024900122

MarkJoy Publishing LLC
P. O. BOX 73741
Houston, TX 77273

Printed in the United States of America

Publisher's Cataloging-in-Publication data
Names: Irabor, Mark, author.
Title: Life's curves and crossroads : my story / Mark Irabor.
Description: Houston, TX: MarkJoy Publishing LLC, 2024.
Identifiers: LCCN: 2024900122 | ISBN: 979-8-9897932-0-4 (paperback) | 979-8-9897932-1-1 (ebook)
Subjects: LCSH Irabor, Mark. | African American clergy--Texas--Biography. | Clergy--Biography. |
Houston (Tex.)--Biography. | BISAC BIOGRAPHY & AUTOBIOGRAPHY / Memoirs
Classification: LCC BX6455 .I73 2024 | DDC 286/.0924--dc23

Table of Contents

Table of Contents

Table of Contents

Table of Contents

Dedication

"I know the plans and thoughts that I have for you," says the Lord... *"to give you a future and a hope."* Jeremiah 29:11 (AMP)

To my beloved wife, Deborah Joy, a lifetime of love and cherished memories began in 1982, and they continue to flourish with each passing day. Your unwavering support, kindness, and boundless joy have filled our years with immeasurable happiness. Together, we've built a life that's truly exceptional, filled with laughter, shared dreams, and countless adventures. As we journey through the chapters of our love story, I am filled with gratitude for your enduring presence and the promises of a future we eagerly embrace. Here's to us, to our extraordinary life, and the endless possibilities that lie ahead. With all my heart, now and forever.

With my lovely wife, Deborah Joy.

Nigeria in the Sixties: A Decade of Independence and Transformation

In the chronicles of Nigeria's history, the year 1964 stands as a pivotal chapter, marked by a confluence of political, social, and economic events that left an indelible imprint on the trajectory of the young nation. Just four years after gaining independence from British colonial rule in 1960, Nigeria found itself grappling with a complex tapestry of challenges and opportunities. The events of 1964 not only shaped the immediate course of the nation but also laid the groundwork for its future development.

Politically, Nigeria was navigating the intricate landscape of its First Republic in 1964. The political structure was characterized by a federal parliamentary system, with Alhaji Abubakar Tafawa Balewa serving as the Prime Minister and Nnamdi Azikiwe occupying the ceremonial position of President. This era was marked by a delicate balance of power, attempting to harmonize the interests of Nigeria's diverse ethnic and cultural groups.

However, the political stability of the First Republic was severely tested by a constitutional crisis that erupted in the Western Region. The region, one of Nigeria's administrative divisions, became a crucible for intense political rivalries and power struggles among its leaders. The situation reached a boiling point, prompting the declaration of a state of emergency in the Western Region. This crisis underscored the fragility of Nigeria's political landscape in the aftermath of colonial rule, as the nation grappled with the intricacies of governance and power distribution.

Simultaneously, the Northern Region experienced the eruption of the Tiv riots, a series of ethnic clashes that reverberated through the fabric of Nigerian society. The Tiv people, indigenous to the region, clashed with the Hausa-Fulani communities, exposing deep-seated ethnic tensions. Beyond the ethnic dimension, these riots were symptomatic of broader political and economic grievances within the diverse Nigerian populace, reflecting the challenges of fostering unity in a nation characterized by cultural and regional diversity.

While political tensions simmered, 1964 also witnessed significant developments in Nigeria's educational landscape.

Recognizing the pivotal role of education in national development, the government introduced the Universal Primary Education (UPE) policy. This ambitious policy aimed to democratize access to primary education across the country, laying the foundation for future educational advancements. The UPE policy reflected a commitment to addressing the educational disparities that existed among Nigeria's diverse population.

Economically, Nigeria was primarily an agrarian society in 1964, and the government was focused on harnessing the potential of the agricultural sector for economic growth. Initiatives were launched to modernize farming practices, improve infrastructure, and enhance overall productivity in agriculture. The success of these initiatives was seen as crucial for a nation striving to establish a self-sufficient and robust economy post-independence.

Infrastructure development was a key priority during this period. The government embarked on projects aimed at improving transportation, communication, and other essential aspects of the country's infrastructure. These efforts were integral to connecting different regions of the vast nation and fostering economic integration. The development of infrastructure was not only a practical necessity for national progress but also a symbolic expression of Nigeria's ambitions on the global stage.

Internationally, Nigeria was carving out its role in the global arena. As a newly independent nation, it engaged in diplomatic endeavors to solidify its position in the international community. Building alliances, establishing trade relationships, and participating in international forums were critical components of Nigeria's foreign policy agenda in 1964. These diplomatic efforts were indicative of the nation's aspirations to be a significant player on the world stage, seeking recognition and cooperation in the community of nations.

The year 1964 was a crucible for Nigeria — a nation in the throes of post-colonial identity formation and nation-building. The political, social, and economic events of this year were emblematic of the challenges inherent in navigating the complexities of diversity, governance, and development. Despite the trials, Nigeria demonstrated resilience and determination as it forged ahead on its path of self-discovery and progress. The events of 1964, though tumultuous, laid the foundation for the continued evolution of Nigeria as a dynamic and influential player on the African continent and the global stage.

On June 12, 1964, I was born.

Roots of Identity

While my parents hail from Egoro Amede, Ekpoma, in Edo State, I was born in Abeokuta, a city that firmly embeds its name in the rich landscape of Ogun State in southwestern Nigeria. Despite being born in Abeokuta, I proudly recognize myself as an Esan man from Egoro-Amede, Ekpoma, in Edo State. In Nigerian tradition, one's heritage is defined by the ancestral ties of their parents. The story of my life begins in this vibrant city, where the echoes of history resonate through the narrow streets and the air carries the scent of tradition and progress in equal measure.

Abeokuta, meaning "under the rock" in the Yoruba language, owes its name to the monumental Olumo Rock that stands majestically over the city. This rock, with its sprawling caves and crevices, not only serves as a geological wonder but has also become an emblematic symbol of Abeokuta and its resilient people.

My birth in Abeokuta connects me to a heritage that spans generations. The city itself is a microcosm of Nigeria's diverse cultural tapestry, with a harmonious blend of ethnicities, languages, and traditions.

In my early years growing up in Abeokuta meant being surrounded by the rich mosaic of Yoruba culture. Traditional music, marked by the rhythmic beats of talking drums and the resonant tones of local instruments, often filled the air. The vibrant colors of Aso-oke, a traditional Yoruba fabric, adorned people during ceremonies and festivals, transforming the city into a kaleidoscope of hues and patterns. These cultural expressions were not mere adornments; they were the threads that wove together the fabric of daily life, creating an atmosphere that celebrated the essence of being Yoruba.

As a child, I have memories of my mother taking me with her when she went to the market to buy food stuff. The markets of Abeokuta were lively hubs of activity, where the spirit of entrepreneurship thrived. Traders and artisans showcased their goods with pride, and the markets became more than just places to buy and sell; they were communal spaces where stories were exchanged, friendships forged, and the heartbeat of the city could be felt.

The aromas of local delicacies wafted through these markets, tempting passersby with the flavors of jollof rice, amala, ewedu soup, and other culinary delights that define Yoruba cuisine.

Education is a cornerstone of life in Abeokuta, with the city hosting prestigious institutions that contribute to the intellectual growth of its residents and beyond. The Federal University of Agriculture, Abeokuta (FUNAAB), and Moshood Abiola Polytechnic are among the educational institutions that impart knowledge and skills, reflecting the city's commitment to progress and development.

However, my childhood was split growing up in Abeokuta and Ikeja, Lagos. Due to the circumstances of my father's job, we moved from Abeokuta to Lagos.

However, growing up in Abeokuta has imprinted my identity with the indomitable spirit of its people, the richness of its culture, and the weight of its history. The warmth and hospitality of the community have been foundational in shaping my worldview. The stories of resilience passed down through generations, have become a guiding force in navigating life's challenges.

Abeokuta, for me, is not just a geographical location; it is a repository of memories and a cultural heritage that I carry with me on my life's journey. As I navigate the path of life, Abeokuta is one of the places that remains an integral part of my story, an origin that shapes my present and molds my future.

Also, growing up in Ikeja, which is nestled in the heart of Lagos, Ikeja stands as a testament to the vibrant diversity and pulsating life that defines this sprawling metropolis. Growing up in Ikeja was an immersion into a mixture of colors, sounds, and experiences that shaped the very core of my identity.

Among the countless memories that dance through the corridors of my mind, the echoes of my time at Ikeja Primary School and the vibrancy of Ipodo Market stand out as vivid brushstrokes on the canvas of my childhood. I loved it when my father's brother, Uncle Philip would take me to Ipodo Market and walk around telling me stories of the different cultures represented in the market and how Ikeja is the place to be and live. He would buy me a Gala and a bottle of Coca-Cola while we talked about my primary school and the value of getting a good education.

Ikeja Primary School was one of my foundations of learning and friendship. It was not just an educational institution; it was a microcosm of the community, a place where the foundation for a lifelong love of learning was laid. The school's gates, adorned with lively murals and the words "Knowledge is Power," welcomed students into a world where curiosity was nurtured, friendships blossomed, and dreams began to take root. The classrooms, though simple, were filled with the lively chatter of students eager to absorb the wisdom imparted by dedicated teachers.

The creaking wooden desks bore the marks of countless pens and pencils, each etching a story of academic pursuit and discovery. The school compound was a playground of possibilities, where we played games and weaved bonds of friendship that would withstand the test of time.

The teachers, often unsung heroes, were beacons of inspiration. They didn't just teach subjects; they instilled values, encouraged creativity, and sparked a thirst for knowledge. Mrs. Adeyemi, my Math teacher, stands out in my memory as a guiding force, fostering my love for numbers that would become a lifelong passion.

Assemblies in the morning were a communal ritual, an opportunity for the entire school to come together and start the day on a note of unity and purpose. The national anthem echoed through the air, and the daily recitation of the school's motto, "Strive for Excellence," became a mantra that echoed in our hearts long after we graduated.

The annual inter-house sports competition was a highlight, transforming the school field into a carnival of colors and athleticism. Students donned their house colors with pride, competing fiercely in events that ranged from track and field to traditional dance. The roar of encouragement from parents and the infectious energy of the cheering squads created an atmosphere of camaraderie that transcended the competition itself.

Ipodo Market resonated with a symphony of sights, sounds, and aromas. Stretching beyond the confines of the school gates, the lively canvas of Ikeja unfolded into the bustling Ipodo Market. More than just a marketplace, Ipodo Market thrived as a living, breathing entity, pulsating with the vibrant rhythm of commerce and culture. Intertwined with the very fabric of daily existence, the market became a sensory banquet, imprinting an enduring impression on all who navigated its maze-like alleys.

The market's display of colors greeted visitors at every turn. Stalls adorned with vibrant fabrics, exotic spices, and fresh produce created a visual spectacle that was both chaotic and captivating. The air was infused with the aroma of roasted plantains, sizzling meats, and the distinctive scent of traditional herbs — a symphony of smells that told the story of the diverse culinary delights available.

Navigating the narrow pathways of Ipodo Market was an adventure in itself. The hustle and bustle of shoppers negotiating prices with animated sellers, the calls of street hawkers peddling their wares, and the occasional burst of laughter from children playing amidst the chaos — all merged into a harmonious cacophony that was uniquely Nigerian.

It was in these crowded alleys that I learned the art

of haggling, a skill that transcended the marketplace and became a metaphor for navigating the challenges of life.

The market was not just a place of commerce; it was a cultural melting pot where people from different backgrounds converged. Yoruba, Igbo, Edo, and Hausa voices blended into a harmonious chorus, showcasing the unity in diversity that characterizes Nigeria. The market was a living testament to the resilience and entrepreneurial spirit of the people, who, amidst the challenges, found a way to thrive and build vibrant communities.

The market became a classroom where I learned about the rich display of Nigerian cuisine, the importance of community, and the resilience of those who made their livelihood amidst the vibrant chaos. It was a place where stories unfolded with every transaction, where the exchange of goods was more than a commercial transaction—it was a cultural exchange, a celebration of shared history and identity.

Just like my early years in Abeokuta growing up in Ikeja was more than a series of events; it was an immersion into a cultural symphony that shaped the very essence of who I am today. Ikeja Primary School laid the academic foundation, nurturing not just intellect but also the values of community, friendship, and the pursuit of excellence. Ipodo Market, with its vibrant colors and dynamic energy, was a microcosm of Nigerian life, teaching lessons of resilience, diversity, and the beauty of shared experiences.

As I reflect on those formative years in Ikeja, I realize that the city wasn't just a backdrop to my childhood; it was an active participant in the narrative of my growth. The lessons learned in the classrooms and marketplaces of Ikeja continue to resonate in my life, serving as a compass that guides me through the intricate tapestry of existence. Ikeja, with its vibrant hues and lively rhythms, is not just a place on the map; it is an integral part of the story that defines who I am—a story that continues to unfold with each passing day.

What's in the Name?

In the story of our lives, our names are the threads that weave the narrative of our existence. They carry stories, traditions, and sometimes unexpected turns of fate. My journey into the realm of nomenclature is a tale that unfolds through the unique and intertwining narratives crafted by my parents. From the unusual choice of "Friday" to the sacred echoes of "Mark," my name bears witness to a confluence of cultural, religious, and personal influences.

The genesis of my name can be traced back to the day of my birth, a Friday, as recounted by my mother. In many cultures, days of the week hold symbolic significance, and most parents in my culture had the names of their male children associated with the day of the week they were born such as Monday, Friday, Saturday, or Sunday which are very popular in my culture. In choosing to name me after the day of my birth, my parents infused a touch of whimsy into the very essence of my identity.

The name "Friday" carries with it a certain spontaneity and lightness, a reminder that life, like the days of the week, unfolds in a series of moments waiting to be embraced.

As the narrative of my name unfolded, it encountered a pivotal chapter at the tender age of three months when I was baptized in the Catholic Church. In the solemnity of the ceremony, the responsibility of naming me took on a sacred dimension. It was here that the pages of my name's story turned, and a new character emerged – "Mark."

The decision to name me Mark was not arbitrary; rather, it was a deliberate choice rooted in religious symbolism. The Catholic priest, a venerable figure in the naming ritual, drew inspiration from the Bible and chose to name me after St. Mark, one of the twelve apostles of Jesus Christ. St. Mark is known for his gospel, a testament to the life and teachings of Jesus, and his name carries a legacy of faith, dedication, and service.

The infusion of "Mark" into my name added layers of meaning; transforming it from a lighthearted choice based on the day of my birth to a name imbued with religious significance. It became a bridge connecting me to a tradition that spans centuries, linking my identity to the stories of saints and the teachings of a faith that has shaped the lives of millions.

In the intersection of "Friday" and "Mark," my name took on a unique duality, a harmonious blend of the playful and the profound. It reflects the fusion of cultural beliefs and religious convictions that are intrinsic to my identity. The juxtaposition of a day of the week with a saint's name symbolizes the tapestry of my existence, woven with threads of both the ordinary and the extraordinary.

My middle name, Irumudomon, was chosen by my Maternal Grandfather. It means, the "Blessings of a Child" in Esan language. Names are not arbitrarily given in my culture; parents put thought into naming children.

The story of my name is not just a tale of linguistic

choices but a reflection of the diverse influences that shape the way we perceive ourselves and how we are perceived by others. It highlights the intricate fabric of human experience, where names transcend being mere labels and instead become vessels carrying the weight of history, culture, and personal narratives.

As I navigate through life as "Mark Irumudomon" I carry with me the legacy of a name that transcends the circumstances of its origin. It is a name that invites curiosity and prompts questions, a name that sparks conversations about the stories behind our identities. In the unique combination of "Mark Irumudomon" I find a name that is not just a label but a living testament to the journey of self-discovery and the myriad influences that shape who we are.

The story of how my parents chose my name is a captivating narrative that spans the realms of cultural whimsy and religious solemnity. My name encapsulates the essence of my identity, a name that weaves together the ordinary and the sacred, the playful and the profound. It is a name that tells a story, a story that continues to unfold with each passing day, adding new chapters to the story of my existence.

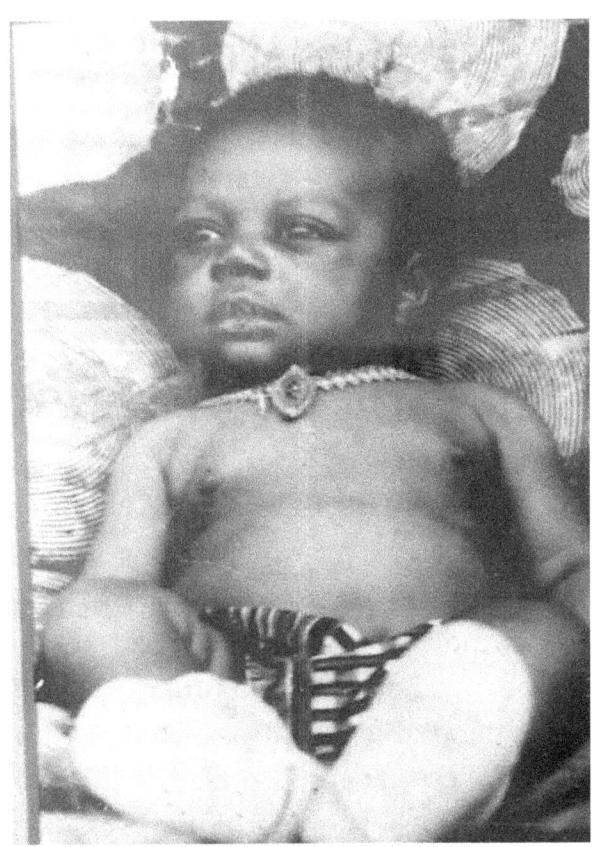

Me at 3 months old.

Growing up in Nigeria

I was born in Abeokuta, Ogun State, Nigeria. My father was a police officer, and my mother was a housewife/businesswoman. She was a housewife first; she took care of the home while she attended to her business interests. Her business was considered secondary by my father and the cultural society's demands.

One vivid memory takes me back to the rhythmic heartbeat of the market in Abeokuta, where the vibrant colors of fruits, vegetables, and assorted goods created a kaleidoscope of sensory delights. Accompanying my mother on these market expeditions was a ritual that unfolded like a cherished chapter of my childhood. The aroma of freshly ground spices, the cacophony of haggling voices, and the palpable energy of commerce are etched into the recesses of my mind.

My father as a police officer was often transferred to different states; the Nigerian police are a national police force and officers are subject to constant transfer. We moved around a lot due to my father's job, going from one station to another in different states. We eventually moved to Ikeja in Lagos State, Nigeria where we lived for a lengthy period. So, my early childhood was spent in Ikeja, Lagos. I went to elementary school (Ikeja Primary School) in Ikeja, Lagos.

It was during this period that the concept of possession and desire took root in my young heart. The chopper bicycle, a coveted possession among the senior officers' children, became a symbol of status and camaraderie. However, my father's reluctance to fulfill this desire left an indelible mark on my memories, a reminder of the bitter taste of unfulfilled yearning that lingered on the palate of my youth.

Even though Lagos was and still is a melting pot with different tribes, the Yoruba people mostly inhabit it. The Yorubas are very cultured, and I love the people, culture, and language.

Yet, amidst the shadows of unmet desires, a radiant figure emerged in the form of Uncle Philip, my father's younger brother. Every payday, Uncle Philip would grace our home with his infectious cheerfulness. As the doors opened to welcome him, the jingling of coins and the crispness of banknotes resonated in the air. With theatrical flair, he would empty his pockets onto the table, declaring the day one of abundance and merriment. "Every day is Christmas! and today we must enjoy" Uncle Philip would declare.

The routine that followed was a delightful script that unfolded with familiarity. Uncle Philip would whisk me away to Ipodo market, a place where stories of Ikeja's diverse culture unfolded like a well-worn narrative. As we strolled through the market's labyrinthine alleys, he regaled me with tales of the people who inhabited this dynamic community. The market became a living, breathing entity, its pulse synchronized with the heartbeat of Ikeja.

On our journey back, Uncle Philip would indulge my youthful cravings, buying me a Gala (meat pie) and a cold Coca-Cola. The crisp flakiness of the pastry, the savory richness of the meat, and the effervescence of the cola formed a trinity of pleasure that transcended the boundaries of taste. These simple indulgences became symbols of Uncle Philip's affection, tangible tokens of his love and the joy he brought into my life.

Uncle Philip was not just a family member; he was the transformer who turned boring moments into golden memories. His presence was a balm for the wounds of unfulfilled desires, a reminder that joy could be found in the simplest of pleasures. His generosity was not confined to material gifts but extended to the invaluable currency of time and attention. As I reflect on these earliest childhood memories, a heart-rending blend of nostalgia and gratitude envelops my heart.

The marketplaces of Abeokuta, the officers' quarters in Ikeja, the unfulfilled desire for a chopper bicycle, and the joyous visits of Uncle Philip—all contribute to the intricate embroidery of my formative years. These memories are not just fragments of the past but pieces of a puzzle that shaped the contours of my identity, connecting me to a time when the world was painted in hues of innocence and wonder.

My father was eventually transferred to Benin City, Bendel State (now Edo State) and we moved to Benin City. Benin City is about an hour's drive to Esan, more especially, Egoro Amede, where my family is from. Moving from Lagos to Benin was hard on me because I had to leave my school and friends behind. The constant moving from one city to another can be hard on kids, especially when they have friends, like I had in school.

Ikeja was a much bigger city than Benin City. Though

I was younger, it seemed like I spent all my life there. I speak Yoruba, which is the main language spoken after the English language, and I missed the friends I had made in Lagos growing up and one in particular – Akeem Fashuba. As an adult, I have always wondered how life has treated him since we lost contact when we left Lagos and moved to Benin City. In Benin City, things were a little different from my point of view as a child.

The culture was far from what I was used to when we lived in Lagos and as I was getting used to the move, my father was transferred again, this time to Igarra, and I had to change schools once again.

While my siblings remained in Benin, I was sent to attend St. Joseph's College, a junior high boarding school in Otuo. Sometimes I wondered how my dad found these schools in rural places. He was not stationed in Otuo, but in Igarra yet, I found myself attending a school in Otuo which was a great distance from Igarra. I did not have any say in the matter, so I just had to obey my father and go. With the transfer to Igarra, my mother and siblings stayed in Benin and my father made the decision that I would go to a new school. This never sat well with me because I preferred to go to school in Benin with my siblings. To this day, I still wonder why I had to leave.

While at Saint Joseph's, my father was transferred to Asaba and again, he decided that I would transfer and attend Saint Patrick's College, a high school in Asaba. His exact words were "If the school was good enough for the former governor of Bendel State (Gov. Ambrose Ali), who attended Saints Patrick's College, it should be good enough for you. You must attend St. Patrick's College!" And I did.

Moving around a lot made it difficult to make and maintain friendships because I did not get a chance to put my roots down anywhere. Nevertheless, I ended up meeting a lifelong friend at Saint Patrick's College. Anthony Mordi (Big Tony) is a lifelong friend who is now an attorney in London. Coincidentally, he lived on the same street as I did in Benin.

I loved growing up in Nigeria. The culture, close extended family ties, the operation of the family system at large, the togetherness, and how people respect their elders are some of the things that I cherish about our Nigerian culture. When I was growing up, children/young adults did not talk back to their elders. You were taught not to talk back to your parents. The task of raising children included respecting others, knowing your place, and the family's expectations of you. The culture demanded it, your neighbors demanded it and oh Lord, your parents demanded it! That was the system I grew up in.

When it came to religion, I grew up in a Christian home. My father was Catholic and he made sure we went to Catholic schools and attended Catholic Church. Not going to the Catholic church on Sundays was like an abomination to him. Going to a church other than a Catholic church to him was a sin. I eventually started going to a non-denominational church because I wanted to know more about the scriptures and the true teachings of the Bible and that was a problem for my father who believed that attendance in a catholic church is synonymous with being a Christian. We did not see eye to eye on this issue and I got into a lot of disagreements with him over not following Catholicism.

Nonetheless, growing up in Nigeria shaped the

way I see the world. I believe that a man not only needs to work hard and care for his immediate family, but it is also his responsibility to care for, help, and lift other family members when he can. However, this assistance should not take away from his ability to care for his immediate family. It also shaped my view on education. It's not a question of if you would go to school, it's a question of what school you would be going to.

There is so much to unpack regarding my upbringing in Nigeria. However, I have mentioned some of the details which impacted me.

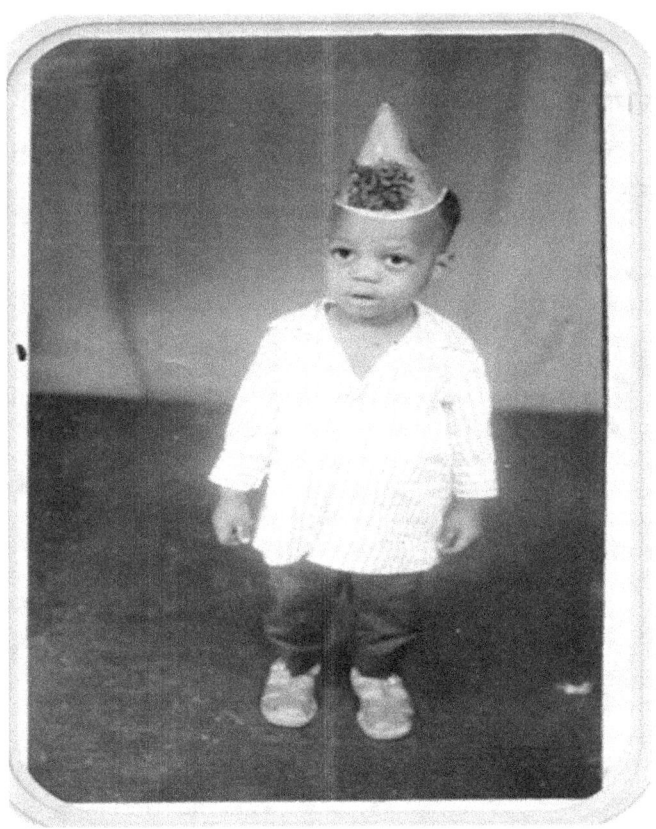

One of my earliest pictures. Seems like I was celebrating something!

I am second from left. I just knew I had style!!!

Reflections on My Childhood Behavior

As a child, my demeanor was characterized by a quiet and reserved nature, setting me apart from the typical exuberance associated with childhood. From a young age, I exhibited a remarkable ability to remain composed and contemplative, providing my parents with a sense of tranquility and assurance that I would not be a source of trouble.

One of the most prominent features of my childhood behavior was my quiet disposition. Unlike many children who are often lively and exuberant, I tended to be more introspective and observant. I wasn't one to engage in boisterous activities or seek attention through exuberant behavior. Instead, I found comfort in the world of my thoughts, exploring my surroundings with a sense of curiosity that was expressed more through quiet observation than through vocalization.

My quiet nature, however, did not imply a lack of engagement or interest in the world around me. On the contrary, I was an avid observer, absorbing information from my environment with a keen sense of awareness. This quiet demeanor allowed me to pick up on nuances that might have gone unnoticed by more outwardly expressive children. It became a tool for learning and understanding, shaping my early experiences and interactions.

While some children may challenge authority or test boundaries, I was inherently respectful and obedient. This made parenting relatively straightforward for my parents, as I rarely ventured into behaviors that required disciplinary action. I understood the importance of rules and boundaries, and I adhered to them conscientiously. My compliance was not out of fear but rather a genuine understanding of the expectations set by my parents.

In addition to being quiet and obedient, focus was a defining trait of my childhood behavior. Once I set my sights on a task or activity, distractions seemed to fade into the background. Whether it was schoolwork, a hobby, or a simple game, I displayed an impressive level of concentration. This focused approach allowed me to excel in academic pursuits and develop skills with a depth that surprised those around me. My parents quickly learned that they could trust me to complete tasks independently and with precision.

This s e n s e of responsibility and focus not only made me a low-maintenance child but also instilled confidence in my parents that they could rely on me to follow through on commitments and responsibilities.

As I navigated the early years of my life, my quiet and focused demeanor became a defining aspect of my personality. I approached challenges with a calm resolve, seeking solutions through careful consideration rather than impulsive action. This thoughtful approach to problem-solving endeared me to teachers and peers alike, creating an environment where collaboration and cooperation flourished.

Despite my introverted tendencies, I forged meaningful connections with a select group of friends who appreciated the depth of my character. In these friendships, my quiet nature was not a hindrance but rather a source of strength, contributing to the harmony of the relationships. As a child, I demonstrated that meaningful connections could be formed not only through constant chatter but also through shared experiences and mutual understanding.

My behavior as a child was characterized by a quiet, focused, and obedient nature. I was not the unruly, trouble-causing child that some parents may encounter.

Instead, I offered a sense of calm and reliability, navigating childhood with a thoughtful approach to learn and interact with the world. My quiet demeanor was not a limitation but a strength that allowed me to forge meaningful connections and excel in various aspects of my early life.

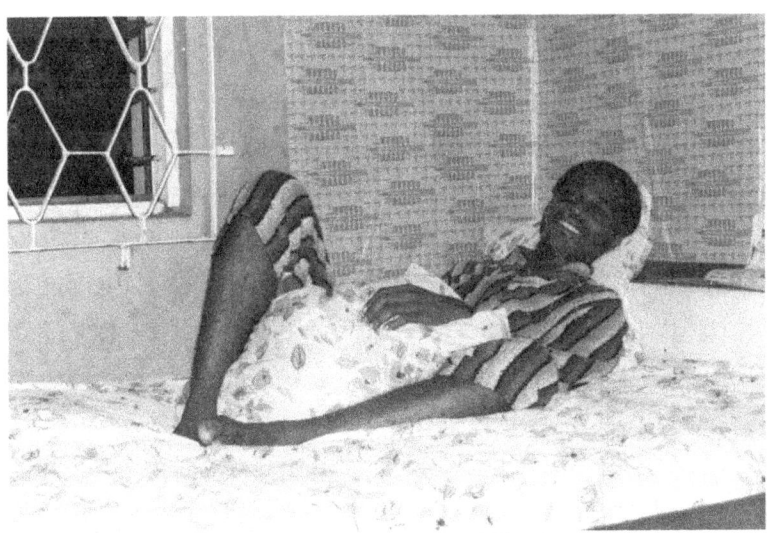

I was really a very quiet person. Most times I would just hang out in my room.

Memories of Childhood Joy: Anticipation and Delight

In the canvas of my early years, particular moments stood out, glittering like gems in the mosaic of growing up. Among the many cherished occurrences, three distinct sources of anticipation colored my childhood with joy.

Every weekend, the air in our home would be charged with excitement as Saturday and Sunday approached. The reason for this palpable anticipation was none other than the arrival of Uncle Philip.

Uncle Philip brought with him an aura of joy that was infectious. His smile could light up the gloomiest of days, and his laughter resonated through the walls of our home.

Uncle Philip was more than a family member; he was a beacon of happiness. The moments leading up to his visits were marked by a sense of eager expectation. I could almost feel the ticking of the clock slowing down as the time drew near for his arrival. The knocking on the door on those weekend afternoons signaled the beginning of a joyous day. There was warmth in his embrace and sincerity in his inquiries about our well-being. Whether he brought small gifts or simply his infectious laughter, Uncle Philip's presence was a treasure that filled our home with happiness.

In a different corner of my childhood memories resided another source of anticipation — the visits to Uncle Egbele's home in Agege, Lagos. It wasn't Uncle Egbele himself that stirred excitement within me but rather the enchanting world his wife (Mama George) cultivated in their yard. A haven for white rabbits nestled in a cage awaited my eager eyes. The sight of those furry creatures, hopping and playing in their enclosed space, was a spectacle that fueled my fascination.

I remember the rhythmic thumping of my heart as I approached the cage, peering through the bars to catch a glimpse of the rabbits' delicate movements. There was an air of mystery surrounding their sheer numbers. I wondered, with curiosity only a child possesses, if Mama George was secretly orchestrating a rabbit sanctuary or if there was a more practical reason behind their presence. The ambiguity only heightened my anticipation during each visit, turning their home into a place of enchantment.

It wasn't just the anticipation of seeing them but the joy of observing their antics that added a unique charm to these visits. Uncle Egbele's home became a haven where the ordinary was transformed into the extraordinary, and each rabbit had a role in this enchanting spectacle.

Beyond the confines of familial visits, another dimension of my childhood anticipation unfolded on the tennis courts. Nestled in the heart of the community, the tennis courts were a hub of activity, attracting individuals from all walks of life. What particularly captured my attention were the senior police officers engaged in spirited games of tennis. The rhythmic thud of the tennis ball, the swish of rackets, and the occasional cheers formed a symphony of athletic prowess.

Watching these seasoned officers gracefully move across the court, executing precise shots with finesse, was akin to witnessing a dance. The court became a stage where strategy and skill intertwined, creating a captivating performance that held my gaze in rapt attention. As a child, the tennis court wasn't merely a recreational space; it was a classroom where the strategies of the game unfolded before my curious eyes.

Each weekend, I eagerly made my way to the tennis courts, armed with the anticipation of witnessing another riveting match. It wasn't just the athleticism that enthralled me; it was the strategic maneuvers, the subtle flicks of the wrist, and the unspoken communication between players that fueled my growing fascination with the sport. The tennis courts became a school of strategy, and I, a willing student absorbing the nuances of a game, went beyond the boundaries of the court.

Looking through my youthful eyes, these moments of anticipation and joy stand out as vivid patches, each contributing to the rich narrative of growing up. Uncle Philip's visits, the enchanting world of white rabbits in Uncle Egbele's yard, and the captivating games on the tennis courts all played a role in shaping the canvas of my childhood. These were not just isolated events; they were threads woven into the fabric of a time when every moment held the promise of something wonderful, and the world was a place of endless discovery and delight.

A Glimpse into My Treasured Books

My favorite books of all time are the Bible and the writings of James Hadley Chase. Each holds a unique significance, offering profound insights and thrilling narratives that have left an indelible mark on my reading journey.

The Bible holds a profound and enduring place in my heart and mind. Its impact transcends time and culture, weaving a rich embroidery of stories, wisdom, and spiritual guidance. My love for the Bible is deeply rooted in its ability to offer a source of solace, inspiration, and moral compass.

At the core of my affection for the Bible is the belief that it is the word of God and it serves as a timeless guide for leading a meaningful and purposeful life. Its narratives, spanning from Genesis to Revelation, provide a roadmap for navigating the complexities of human existence. The stories of Adam and Eve, Noah's Ark, Moses and the Ten Commandments, the life of Jesus Christ, and many others offer profound lessons that resonate across generations.

The Bible serves as a literary masterpiece, captivating with its poetic language, vivid imagery, and powerful metaphors. The Psalms, for example, are a collection of heartfelt expressions that capture the full spectrum of human emotions—from joy and gratitude to despair and longing. The parables of Jesus, simple yet profound, convey profound truths about love, forgiveness, and the nature of the divine.

One of the Bible's most enduring qualities is its ability to provide comfort and solace in times of adversity. The Psalms, in particular, offer a refuge for those grappling with sorrow or uncertainty. The words of Psalm 23 tells us, "The Lord is my shepherd; I shall not want."(KJV) They have provided solace to countless souls navigating the challenges of life. In times of despair, turning to the Bible becomes a source of strength and a reminder of enduring hope.

Beyond its narrative and poetic elements, the Bible is a treasure trove of wisdom literature. The Book of Proverbs, for instance, is a collection of practical insights on living a virtuous and righteous life. Its verses offer guidance on topics ranging from the value of hard work to the importance of humility. The wisdom literature in the Bible transcends religious boundaries, offering timeless principles that resonate with people of diverse backgrounds and beliefs.

My love for the Bible is also rooted in its transformative power. The stories of individuals who experienced profound personal transformation — such as the Apostle Paul's journey from persecutor to apostle — inspire a belief in the possibility of redemption and change. The Bible challenges individuals to examine their lives, confront their shortcomings, and strive for a higher moral and spiritual plane.

The teachings of Jesus, central to the New Testament, embody a radical message of love, compassion, and forgiveness. The Sermon on the Mount, with its emphasis on humility, mercy, and peacemaking, stands as a revolutionary manifesto for a life centered on love for God and love for one's neighbor. The Golden Rule, encapsulated in Matthew 7:12, epitomizes a universal ethic that transcends cultural and religious boundaries: "So whatever you wish that others would do to you, do also to them." (KJV)

As a source of moral guidance, the Bible addresses the fundamental questions of human existence. Its ethical teachings provide a framework for navigating the complexities of right and wrong, offering a moral compass that transcends cultural relativism. The Ten Commandments, etched in the moral the consciousness of Judeo-Christian traditions outlines fundamental principles for ethical living.

The Bible's historical accounts, while rooted in a specific time and place, offer timeless lessons about the consequences of human choices and the unfolding of divine providence. The Exodus narrative, for example, speaks to the themes of liberation, justice, and the enduring promise of a land flowing with milk and honey.

The historical accounts in the Bible, whether recounting the rise and fall of empires or the struggles of individuals, illuminate the human condition with depth and insight that transcends mere historical documentation.

My love for the Bible extends beyond religious affiliation; it is a love for the profound insights, timeless wisdom, and transformative power captured within its pages. It is a recognition of the enduring impact that this sacred text has had on individuals, societies, and cultures throughout the ages. Whether studied for its literary brilliance, moral teachings, or spiritual guidance, the Bible stands as a testament to the enduring power of words to shape hearts, minds, and souls. In its pages, I find not only a source of inspiration but a guiding light that illuminates the path toward a life of purpose, compassion, and spiritual fulfillment.

On a completely different note, the works of James Hadley Chase take me into the gritty and suspenseful world of noir fiction. Chase, a prolific British author, became synonymous with gripping narratives, intricate plots, and morally ambiguous characters.

One of his most famous works, "The Big Sleep," introduces readers to the iconic detective Philip Marlowe. The novel's dark and atmospheric setting, coupled with Marlowe's sharp wit, creates a captivating noir experience.

"The Guilty Are Afraid" is another gripping novel by James Hadley Chase that explores the darker realms of human nature. Set against a backdrop of crime and deception, the story unfolds with suspense and intrigue. The title itself hints at the pervasive theme of guilt and fear that haunts the characters throughout the narrative.

Chase, known for his skill in crafting compelling crime fiction, weaves a tale of moral ambiguity and psychological tension. The characters grapple with their conscience and the consequences of their actions, creating a web of suspense that keeps me on the edge of my seat.

The narrative delves into the complexities of crime and punishment, examining the emotional toll on those involved in illicit activities. Chase masterfully develops the plot, revealing unexpected twists and turns that challenge conventional notions of right and wrong.

"The Guilty Are Afraid" is not merely a crime novel; it's a psychological exploration that forces readers to confront the darker aspects of the human psyche. As the characters navigate the treacherous waters of guilt and fear,

Chase skillfully builds a narrative that captivates and leaves me with a lasting impression on the understanding of morality and human nature.

Chase's writing is characterized by a keen understanding of human psychology and a flair for creating compelling antiheroes. His characters are often morally complex, navigating a world filled with crime, deception, and moral ambiguity. In "No Orchids for Miss Blandish," for example, Chase explores the criminal underworld, presenting a world where right and wrong are not easily distinguishable.

What fascinates me about James Hadley Chase's writing is his skill in portraying the darker aspects of human nature. He delves into the complexities of crime and punishment, examining the thin line between the law and those who defy it. Chase's ability to blend suspense with social commentary adds depth to his novels, elevating them beyond mere entertainment.

Both the Bible and Chase's works explore the complexities of morality and the consequences of human actions. While the Bible offers spiritual guidance and moral principles, Chase's novels present a more nuanced perspective, where characters grapple with their moral compass in a world tainted by crime and corruption.

Additionally, the themes of redemption and forgiveness, central to many biblical stories, find echoes in Chase's narratives. His characters, despite their flaws and misdeeds, often undergo transformative journeys, seeking redemption or, in some cases, grappling with the consequences of their choices.

The Bible, with its timeless wisdom and spiritual depth, has provided me solace and guidance in moments of reflection. On the other hand, James Hadley Chase's noir fiction has taken me on thrilling rides through the shadows of human nature, challenging my perceptions and keeping me hooked until the last page.

Learning to Ride a Bicycle

Learning to ride a bicycle is a rite of passage for many, a skill that symbolizes newfound freedom and independence. My journey into the world of cycling began with a simple desire and a deal struck with my Uncle Joel. Little did I know that this venture would not only teach me how to ride a bicycle but also impart valuable life lessons about perseverance and determination.

It all started when I expressed my eagerness to learn how to ride a bicycle to my Uncle Joel, who happened to own one. He agreed to help me achieve this goal, but not without a condition – I had to clean up his house in exchange for the privilege of using his bicycle. Excitement coursed through me at the prospect of finally acquiring this essential skill, and with a sense of determination, I agreed to the terms.

As my uncle brought out his bicycle, I envisioned a traditional teaching scenario where he would guide me through the process.

However, my expectations were swiftly dispelled when he simply handed me the bicycle and instructed me to go learn on my own. His parting words were both encouraging and cautionary, as he warned me that falling was inevitable but getting back up was the key to mastering the art of cycling.

With a mix of apprehension and excitement, I

climbed onto the bicycle for my first attempt. The initial moments were disastrous; my lack of balance became immediately apparent as I found myself repeatedly tumbling to the ground. It felt like I was walking the bicycle more than riding it, and frustration threatened to overtake my determination. However, the memory of the promised reward and the desire to conquer this challenge propelled me forward.

Undeterred by the setbacks of my first attempt, I returned to the bicycle the following week for another try. The outcome was disappointingly similar – more falls, more frustration, and seemingly little progress. Despite the initial struggles, I persevered, convincing myself that every fall was a step closer to success. My uncle's words echoed in my mind: "Get back on the bicycle and keep riding."

As the weeks passed, my determination grew stronger. Each fall became a lesson, a stepping stone toward achieving balance and control. My third attempt marked a turning point. After countless bruises and aching limbs, I finally found the delicate equilibrium needed to stay atop the bicycle. The sense of accomplishment was exhilarating, and I reveled in the newfound freedom of riding without constant falls.

From that moment on, the bicycle became my trusted companion. I spent hours navigating the neighborhood streets, honing my skills, and relishing the wind in my hair. The lessons learned extend beyond the physical act of riding – I discovered the power of resilience, the importance of facing challenges head-on, and the sweet taste of success earned through hard work.

Learning to ride a bicycle may seem like a simple task, but the journey I undertook was a profound experience of self-discovery. It taught me that success often requires perseverance in the face of adversity, that setbacks are merely stepping stones to achievement, and that the sweetest victories are those earned through personal effort.

In retrospect, I am grateful for my Uncle Joel's unconventional teaching method. By entrusting me with the responsibility of learning independently, he instilled in me a sense of self-reliance and resilience. The process of teaching myself to ride a bicycle not only enriched my life with a valuable skill but also became a metaphor for tackling life's challenges with determination and unwavering resolve.

As I look back on that pivotal moment in my life, I can't help but appreciate the transformative power of perseverance and the invaluable lessons learned through the simple act of riding a bicycle. The journey was not just about mastering a physical skill; it was a journey of self-discovery that shaped my outlook on challenges and instilled in me a lifelong commitment to facing them head-on, no matter how many times I might fall.

My Dad's Story

Thinking over my childhood, I have so many wonderful memories of my dad. Sir Joseph Abumere Irabor, my dad, was born on August 22, 1935, to the family of Mr. Omoike Irabor and Mrs. Otue Irabor Nee Otue Ehiehoya (my grandparents) of Uwenbo both of Egoro Amede in Esan West local government area in Edo State, Nigeria. At the end of World War II, the colonial occupiers-imposed taxation on villagers. In addition, they required at least one child to be registered in school. My dad was first enrolled at St. Michael's Catholic School in Egoro Eguare and was later sent to St. Gregory's Catholic School in Ekpoma for his elementary education which he completed in 1952.

At the end of his elementary education in 1952, he left Egoro Amede for Lagos to live with some of his relatives. All efforts for him to enroll in secondary school were not successful due to financial constraints. As a result, he was forced to go to work; he began doing day labor work as a bricklayer and other odd jobs while he was taking overseas correspondence classes for his secondary education. Upon successful completion of his secondary education, he enlisted in the Nigerian Police Force on July 1, 1955. He underwent a rigorous six-month training program at the Police College in Ikeja, Lagos.

At the end of his training, he had to wait for two months to be posted to his assigned station due to Queen Elizabeth's II visit to Nigeria, which was still under the colonization of the British government). After her visit, my dad was posted to work in Abeokuta the capital of Ogun State (where I was born). After a few years, he was transferred back to Ikeja, Lagos where he worked in all sectors of the force, and he continued to take correspondence courses which eventually led to his promotion to Superior Police Officer (SPO).

Even as an SPO, he continued taking courses in Nigeria and overseas and was invited to attend the Metropolitan Police College in Hendon, London. He did very well in his courses. He was at the top of his class and was asked to stay as a permanent instructor at one of their police colleges. He declined and opted to return to Nigeria.

In 1973, he was transferred to Benin City in the old Bendel State (now Edo and Delta States). Upon arriving in Benin City, he was transferred to Akoko-Edo local government area as a Divisional Police Officer (DPO) during the Ikeregbe Drum crisis. There was a fifteen-year chieftaincy dispute, and my dad was to help resolve the ongoing dispute. After that, he was transferred to the Oshimili Local Government area where there was, once again, a traditional dispute between the old East Central and Bendel State. This dispute was resolved constitutionally. He then worked in various areas throughout Nigeria.

I remember when we lived in Ikeja, Lagos, and we moved from the barracks to the officer's quarter. My dad was first promoted to the rank of Assistant Superintendent of Police (ASP). He was very happy. The flat (as it was called) was nice and spacious. He worked in different divisions and was eventually assigned to teach and train police recruits at the Police College in Ikeja, Lagos. The job of training future officers was an advancement since only the educated and promising policemen were selected for the teaching position. The annual parade that was conducted at the Police College was an event that everyone looked forward to attending. Senior police officers would attend such as the commandants and commissioners of police. My dad always had his white costumed officer's uniform-type jacket on, and he looked good in it. He rose in rank and retired as a police commissioner on August 8, 1990.

While my dad was a very hard-working man, he was an extremely complicated man; he would try to help everyone to a fault. He spent more time helping and guiding other people to achieve their dreams and never at any time provided the same guidance to me. He believed that if he provided food and shelter his job would be done. At no time did he ever sit down with me and ask what my dreams were or my plans. I had to figure it all out by myself thus, I had to grow up fast and educate myself on a lot of life's issues.

My dad was a hard-working man who worked his way out of poverty. He helped shape my work ethic of putting in an honest day's work. Everything he had, he worked for. No one ever gave him anything and he never asked anyone for anything. He simply lived within his means. He would take me to the farm and show me how to work on the farm (I wasn't always enthusiastic about this).

Some of the things he said to me as a child stuck with me to this day such as "I have never met a serious person that went to bed before 10:00 pm and is still asleep after 5:00 am." Growing up I had to wake up at 5:00 am to wash his car daily. Up to this day, I am awake at 5:00 am. I didn't see the value of these lessons then but now as an adult, I understand he wanted to build my character. He wanted me and all my siblings to get a good education. He was an example of a person who worked hard to support his family. He loved his job with the Nigerian Police, cherished his church. and the organizations he was a member of.

After my Dad retired, he visited us in the United States, and I had the opportunity to get to know him on another level. He shared in many important events in our life such as getting my doctorate in Florida, my son's wedding and just visiting to be near the family.

On many occasions, he spoke fondly of his trip to London during his days with the police. He enjoyed his time and shared many stories with me. On one visit, we drove to Gulfport, Mississippi to show Dad the casinos and the beach. We made a stop at the outlet mall and went into the Van Heusen store to look around. My Dad stopped in his tracks and looked around amazed. "A whole store of Van Heusen shirts? I don't believe this!" I looked surprised but my Dad began to recount a story from his past.

During the early days in the police department, one of the commandant's wives had traveled to London on holiday. While there she saw Van Heusen shirts. Upon returning to Nigeria, she urged her husband to have the men wear Van Heusen shirts because they looked so nice. As a result, the Commandant gave an order for the men to begin wearing this type of shirt only. Well, they did not sell the shirts in Nigeria and the men were baffled. So, they had to scrape money together to send one man to London to purchase the shirts! It was a big problem. Now he was in a store that sold a lot of Van Heusen shirts! We all laughed when hearing the story, especially the gleam in my Dad's eye as he told the story.

Above all, my dad was a good man, and he did the absolute best he knew. We had a big party for his 80th birthday and I witnessed the immense love people had for him. He was highly respected, and people saw him as a man of great integrity and dignity.

He died on August 21, 2016, at the age of eighty-one. A day shy of his eighty-second birthday.

Daddy and I in 2015

Daddy, second from the left in his Senior Officer's uniform during official occasions.

On the left: Daddy in his uniform. On the right: Daddy and his friend. He was a handsome young man. Some say I am his mirror image. What do you think?

Daddy and Mommy look wonderful!

Strength of a Mother

My mother, Mrs. Beatrice Omonivie Ojo Irabor, was born into the family of Mr. Aigboruan Ojo and Mrs. Anumen Ojo from Egoro Amede, Ekpoma in Esan West local government area in Edo State, Nigeria. She is the eldest daughter of her parents but, the fifth of eight children. She had four older brothers and three younger sisters. My mother was not the typical housewife because she was involved in a lot of businesses while at the same time taking care of her children.

After my father's promotion, my mother would get up very early in the morning to attend to her business of frying buns, making pies, and selling boiled eggs. The police recruits were her main customers, and they would line up to buy buns and pies from her. It was not an easy business sitting by the wood fire and frying buns and pies as early as 5:00 am.

She was a very industrious person. She did not stop there but continued with other businesses. She started a popcorn factory where she mass-produced popcorn for delivery to local business people for their stores.

She was also a distributor of Coca-Cola products, building cement, and beer (Guinness, Star Larger and Heineken). On several occasions, I made product deliveries for her using her brand-new light blue Peugeot 505 pickup truck.

I loved driving that truck. I used to drive the vehicle to supply my mother's customers.

Coming home during school holidays, I spent a lot of time with my mother reminiscing about her upbringing, talking about her dad, my grandfather. She loved talking about her father, especially how she could have gotten better educated. However, her father's decision not to send her to school was influenced by his uncles.

As a young girl, she wanted to be a nurse. She and a friend from our village applied and took the entrance nursing exam to attend Izuma Memorial Hospital Nursing School in Irrua. Her dreams were dashed by her father's uncles who convinced her father not to allow her to attend nursing school. They said the school was too far for a girl to be sent to. During her time of growing up, young ladies were expected to get married and have children and not think about education. She always felt shortchanged not advancing her education. She thought with time she could convince him to change his mind but, he died before her dream of getting a higher education could be realized.

On the contrary, she spoke very little of her mother. She doesn't say much about her mother, only that she was a nice person. My mother is a very loving person; she was incredibly supportive through the process of my leaving Nigeria to come and study in the United States.

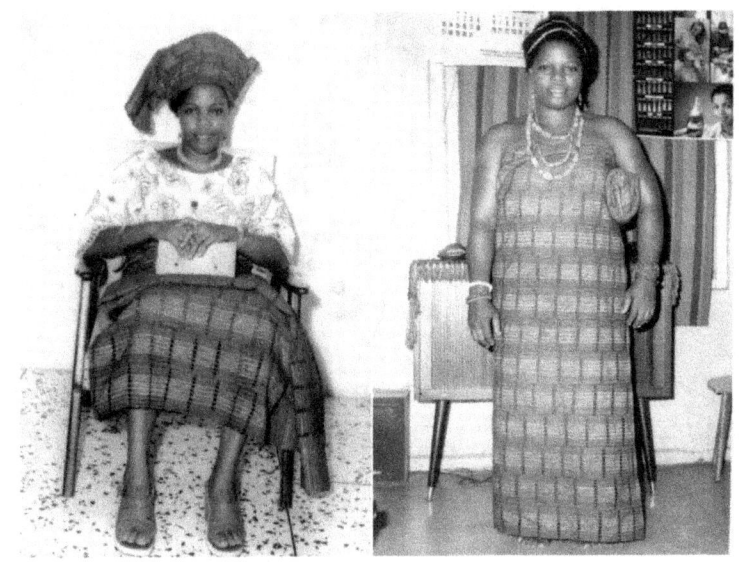

Mommy in her younger days; she looked so beautiful! On the right Mommy is standing in front of our first Sanyo black & white television.

Daddy, Mama Umolu (Mommy's cousin) and Mommy

Mommy, my little brother Darlington, and I in Nigeria

Mama Frances Ford, Me, and Mommy at MI 3 Center,
Houston, Texas. I am so blessed.

Roots and Branches: My Grandparents' Story

I was not fortunate enough to have the memory of my grandparents, either on my father's side or my mother's side.

However, in one of his writings to me, my father told me that his father and mother, Omoike Irabor and Otue Irabor (nee Ehiehoya) were peasant farmers, and due to difficult circumstances, they added pear (the fruit) trading to their work to cope with the harsh conditions brought on by the British missionaries during Nigeria's colonization. During World War I, the colonial masters-imposed taxation on all male adults in the villages which hindered their progress and affected their way of life. The little money they were making to survive now, a portion had to be paid in taxation to help support the British during the war. Before the imposition of the taxation on all male adults, they were able to feed themselves and their families with the crops harvested from their farms. Not only was the taxation imposed, but it was also recklessly administered by the traditional chiefs and elders of the villages. Failure to pay the imposed taxation on time was met with suspension of farming rights and imprisonment; it made life difficult for everyone at that time.

On the positive side, the missionaries required that at least one child from each family must be sent to school, but they also imposed school fees which made it more difficult for them. Though the school fees were minimal it was difficult to get so my grandfather, in addition to farming and pear trading, had to spend two to three days at a time in the bush to cut local leaves that were used to roof houses to sell.

On my mother's side, my grandfather was also a farmer. Aigboruan Ojo planted and harvested the best yams that can be found in our village, and everybody came to him to buy yams. I have a picture of my grandfather from my mother's side of the family, but I don't have a picture of either of my grandmothers or grandfather from my father's side of the family. Thinking about them and the life they lived saddens me, but it was not something that I had the power to change. My mother never talked about her mother, Alume Ojo, either. I often asked her what her mother was like, and she did not talk a lot about her. However, her eyes light up when she talks about her father, how he was a great farmer, and how she felt loved by him.

I was fortunate to have had a great aunt that we looked up to as a grandmother. Mama Roslyn Eroh was beautiful, quiet, and had a good spirit. She loved us and we loved her too. I remember she had a store in front of her house where she sold provisions. I loved going to her store sitting down and having long conversations with her. She was a lovely lady; she passed on a few years ago. I do miss her. I am glad that I was blessed with the opportunity to be able to travel to Nigeria for her funeral to pay my respects.

I also had a great uncle (my grandfather's brother)

who always visited us when we lived in Lagos. In the early evenings, he would have all the children sit in a circle and he would tell us stories. His stories were wild; they made you travel with imagination upon his every single word. He always told the stories in our native language, starting with "Once Upon a time, there was a turtle, there was a tiger, and there was a rat, and they tried to outsmart each other." I have a faint memory of him, but I remember some of the stories he told us when we were children. He was a great storyteller.

I wish I knew my grandparents. My children are so fortunate that they had a chance to meet their grandparents. I thank God for that because it makes a difference in one's life, knowing where you come from beyond your parents. Every time I see any of my children or any of my grandchildren my eyes light up and my heart is filled with joy. I can't wait for a hug! I believe my grandparents were good people despite not having a memory of them.

From Left: Mama Umolu, Me, Uncle Sylvester Ojo and Mama Eroh
(she was like a grandmother to me)

I wished that life was not so harsh for them, being that they were farmers and the conditions they lived in were arduous.

My Grandfather, Mr. Aigboruan Ojo

Nine Voices, One Family

Growing up in a large family of nine children, with five boys and four girls, was an adventure like no other. I held the position of the second child and the oldest son, a role that carried a hefty load of expectations and responsibilities. In the Nigerian culture, large families are not uncommon, and our household was always brimming with life. There were not only my siblings but also extended family, cousins, aunts, uncles, and even adopted family members. It was a lively bunch, and we thrived amid all the chaos.

Being the eldest son meant that I was looked up to by my younger siblings, and it came with a sense of responsibility that began at a young age. I was expected to set an example, help with chores, and lend a hand in taking care of the younger ones. From cooking to cleaning, my parents instilled in me the values of hard work and a strong work ethic. I took on these tasks with pride, as I knew they were contributing to the well-being of our family.

Growing up in a large family had its perks, but it also required me to grow up fast and learn a lot about life lessons on my own. Being the second child and the eldest son meant I had to take on responsibilities from a young age, and these experiences shaped me in profound ways.

As the eldest son, I often found myself in situations

where I needed to be self-reliant. I vividly remember the day I decided to learn how to ride a bike. While some of my friends had their parents guiding them, I had to figure it out on my own. With determination and a few scraped knees, I eventually mastered the art of balancing on two wheels. It was a valuable lesson in perseverance and independence.

Teaching myself to ride a bike was just the beginning. As I grew older, I realized that I needed to learn even more important life skills. One of the most significant milestones in my journey to adulthood was teaching myself how to drive. I had to rely on my resourcefulness.

I borrowed my father's car and slowly began to familiarize myself with the basics of driving. I had to wash the car every morning. I watched my father very carefully while he was driving. So, each morning, I began to move the car around. It was a daunting experience. I made countless mistakes along the way, from stalling at intersections to narrowly avoiding minor accidents. But with each mistake, I learned and improved.

Self-teaching how to drive not only gave me a sense of accomplishment but also taught me about responsibility and the consequences of my actions. I had to be accountable for my mistakes and constantly adapt to the challenges that came my way.

In our household, there were always people around, and it wasn't limited to just our immediate family. We frequently hosted extended family gatherings, and our home became a hub of activity during holidays and celebrations. The sound of laughter, chatter, and the aroma of delicious Nigerian dishes filled the air. These gatherings reinforced the significance of family bonds and taught us the importance of unity.

Despite the occasional squabbles and disagreements that are bound to occur among siblings, we were a close-knit group. Our relationships were built on a foundation of trust and unconditional love. Our parents, who were the pillars of our family, emphasized the values of respect and support for one another.

One of the cherished memories of our family was the storytelling sessions. While growing up in Lagos, my great-uncle, during his visits would gather us in a circle, and we would listen to enchanting tales about our ancestors, their struggles, and their triumphs. These stories not only kept our culture alive but also instilled a deep sense of pride in our heritage.

Visits from extended family members, cousins, aunts, uncles, and even adopted family members were common occurrences. These visits were eagerly anticipated, as they reinforced the importance of maintaining strong connections with relatives. We would spend hours catching up, sharing stories, and celebrating each other's achievements.

As the years passed, our family continued to grow, welcoming new members through birth and marriage. The sense of unity and the values instilled in us by our parents remained unwavering. We learned that family is not just about blood but about the bonds that are formed through love, respect, and shared experiences.

Growing up in a large family was a privilege, and I wouldn't have had it any other way. It taught me the importance of responsibility, the value of unity, and the significance of cherishing family bonds. Our lively household, filled with love and laughter, will forever hold a special place in my heart, reminding me of the beauty of a closely-knit family in the rich tapestry of Nigerian culture.

Family

Family Vacations Are Not All the Same

As a young child growing up in Nigeria, the concept of a family vacation carried an entirely different meaning compared to the typical Western notion of beach resorts, historical landmarks, and museums. In my early years, family vacations weren't characterized by exotic destinations or elaborate travel plans; rather, they revolved around the simplicity of spending more time at home, engaging in chores during school holidays, and accompanying my father to the farm. It was a unique perspective shaped by cultural nuances, economic constraints, and personal experiences.

Unlike the stereotypical family vacations portrayed in glossy brochures and Hollywood films, where families embark on adventures to picturesque locales, my childhood in Nigeria was grounded in a more pragmatic and locally influenced understanding of leisure time. The idea of jetting off to tropical paradises or exploring ancient ruins simply didn't feature in our family narrative. Instead, the essence of a vacation was found in the familiar surroundings of home and the communal rhythms of daily life.

School holidays marked a departure from the routine, but it wasn't an escape to distant lands. Instead, it meant plunging into a different set of activities. The extended break from classes was an opportunity to engage in productive pursuits, with an emphasis on shared responsibilities within the family. Chores became the hallmark of our vacations, transforming our home into a hub of activity. Cleaning, organizing, and maintaining the household were integral parts of the holiday experience, fostering a sense of collaboration and shared purpose.

For me, the highlight of these vacations extended beyond the confines of home. I actively participated in helping my mother with her businesses; also delivering popcorn and beer to her customers. Additionally, I accompanied my father to the farm. The expansive fields, teeming with life and possibilities, became my playground. While other children might have been building sandcastles on a beach or exploring parks, I was cultivating a connection to the earth, learning the fundamentals of agriculture, and understanding the cycles of nature.

As I reflect on those early years, I realize that our family vacations were not defined by the places we visited but by the lessons we learned.

In a global context, the concept of family vacations varies widely, shaped by cultural backgrounds and economic circumstances. While some may associate vacations with luxury resorts and sightseeing tours, for others, it might involve reconnecting with ancestral roots, engaging in traditional practices, or simply finding solace in the familiarity of home.

In Nigeria, where economic considerations often play a pivotal role in shaping lifestyles, the notion of an ideal vacation diverges from the Western standard. The emphasis on community, family ties, and practical engagements reflects a cultural ethos that places value on collective well-being over individual pursuits. It's a perspective that challenges the conventional narrative surrounding vacations, urging a reevaluation of what truly constitutes a meaningful and fulfilling break from the routine.

With time, I found opportunities to embark on journeys that transcended the borders of my hometown. These experiences exposed me to the richness of cultural diversity, historical marvels, and the sheer beauty of the world. It was a transformative period that expanded my understanding of what vacations could entail while allowing me to carry the values of community, responsibility, and simplicity from my childhood in new and unfamiliar settings.

Family vacations, I discovered, are not confined to a specific geography, or set of activities. They are a dynamic and evolving concept that adapts to the changing landscapes of our lives.

From the simplicity of rural life in Nigeria to the grandeur of international adventures, each iteration contributes to a more comprehensive understanding of the multifaceted nature of vacations.

My journey from childhood vacations in Nigeria to the exploration of global landscapes has been a testament to the transformative power of perspective. What started as a local and pragmatic approach to leisure time evolved into a broader, more inclusive understanding of the world. Family vacations, for me, no longer carry a singular definition but represent a mosaic of experiences that celebrate the diversity of cultures, values, and landscapes that shape our lives.

Memories and Milestones:
High School Friends
Forever

When I graduated from high school, we did not have access to social media. Unfortunately, I lost contact with many of my high school classmates; especially since I did not live in the same town that I graduated high school from. I attended high school as a boarding student. I lived on campus while I was in school, and my family lived in Benin City about three hours in driving distance.

After high school, everyone went their separate ways. Most of my high school classmates moved to other cities to seek employment while others furthered their education by attending Universities all around the country. A small percentage of my high school classmates traveled overseas to places like London (which was a popular destination for those who could afford it). Of course, I left for the United States to further my education.

However, I am in contact with one of my high school classmates, Anthony Mordi, whom I consider not just as a friend but a brother to this day. We lived a few blocks from each other on the same street in Benin City. He attended and graduated with a Bachelor of Arts degree from the University of Benin. He then continued his education by going to law school in London. He is now a respected practicing attorney in London, England. With me living in the United States and him in England we do not see each other as much but we keep the line of communication going.

Regarding my high school experience, it was ok. I started at Saint Joseph High School in Otuo, previously known as Azama College. The school was on a hill with a beautiful landscape. Many of the teachers at the school were Indian expatriates and they were the math and science teachers. At St. Joseph's College, I participated in sports like soccer and tennis. I represented my school in the Regional Junior Division Tennis Tournament. I have always enjoyed playing tennis as it gives me a way to relax from the arduous class schedules. One thing that I did not like was that we had to walk a good distance to fetch water from the stream or river since the school did not have a good water supply when I attended. I spent two years at St. Joseph's and transferred to St. Patrick's after my father was transferred to Asaba.

St. Patrick's College in Asaba during my time there was like a military-style school with tight scheduling. Our wake-up time was 5 am. Then you are required to fix your bed, and get ready for breakfast and after that, we assemble at the front of the administrative building by class in a single-line format for roll call. Classes began at 8:00 am. We would march to our classes. Classes ended around 4:00 pm and then we had our leisure time for about one hour. Study time began at 5:00 pm. We were then allowed one and a half hours for sports time (of your choice) before dinner time in the cafeteria. Dinner started at 6:30 pm and ended at 7:30 pm.

On Saturdays, there were a lot of social events and sports that one can participate in such as soccer, tracks, tennis, religious services, and club activities like the Bible Study Group which I was a member. I looked forward to the weekly services, which provided me with a terrific opportunity to learn the scriptures. I eventually enrolled in the Bible knowledge classes for three straight years where we explored stories in the bible from Genesis to Revelation.

At St. Patrick's College everyone was expected to work at the farm since the school is self-sufficient and food harvested from the farm was also cooked for the students. The school had a big chicken poultry that produced eggs cooked on Sunday mornings.

Corn, yam, and other vegetable products were all planted and harvested on the farm. Going to the farm is something I did not enjoy but everyone had to have farm time on their class schedule.

St Patrick's College campus was even more beautiful than St. Joseph's campus. While St. Joseph's was in a rural area, St Patrick's was in a city and a lot of prominent Nigerians had attended the school. The school was well-staffed, and the science labs were well-equipped. I enjoyed my time at the school and tried different sports like high jump and huddles but was not good at them. In the case of huddles after several tries and hitting my legs on the huddle, I gave that up since I knew that I was not good at it. So, I decided to stick to what I was good at like tennis and soccer.

While I enjoyed my time at St. Joseph's and St. Patrick's, I wanted to attend school in Benin City where my family lived. Some of my cousins also attended school in

Benin, but my dad insisted on having me attend a boarding school far from home. To this day, I do not understand my father's motivation in having me attending schools so far from where our family lived in Benin City. I resented that for a long time because I felt he could have allowed me to attend high school in Benin or in Esan where I could have learned more about my cultural heritage at a much younger age.

My high school days at SPC Asaba were fun.

Top Picture: Anthony Mordi, my childhood friend, will always be my brother. In London, England, September 2022.

Bottom Picture: Anthony Mordi, Me, and Peter Ejiofor, all high school classmates, had fun at SPC Asaba. Here we are in London, England, September 2022.

Learning to Drive: A Self-Taught Journey Through observation and Practice

Learning to drive is a significant milestone in one's life, a rite of passage that symbolizes independence and freedom. For me, this journey was unconventional, as I took it upon myself to master the art of driving by closely observing my father. His car, a manual five-speed drive, became my training ground, and through a combination of attentive observation and daring experimentation, I managed to teach myself how to drive.

My father's car, an off-white Peugeot 504 CL was not an automatic transmission; it was a manual transmission, adding an extra layer of complexity to the learning process. Manual cars require a hands-on approach, with the driver actively engaging with the gears to control the vehicle's speed and power. As I watched my father effortlessly navigate through traffic, smoothly shifting gears, and maintaining control of the car, I became increasingly fascinated by the intricate dance between man and machine.

My first real interaction with the car came as part of my daily chores – washing my father's car. It was during these moments that I would observe him most closely. Every gear change, every turn, and every interaction with traffic became a lesson. I paid attention to the details of his movements, the rhythm of gear shifts, and the coordination required to navigate the streets confidently.

One day, after completing my usual car-washing duties, I decided to take a bolder step. Instead of simply moving the car to a different spot, as my father preferred, I opted to take it for a short drive down the street. The pretense was that I was warming up the engine and preparing the car for him, but in reality, I was driven by a desire to test my increasing driving skills.

As I eased the car down the familiar streets, I felt a surge of excitement mixed with nervousness. The responsibility of handling a vehicle was daunting, but the thrill of autonomy was invigorating. I carefully mimicked the actions I had observed countless times from the passenger seat – the precise movements of the clutch, the deliberate shifts of the gears, and the calculated acceleration and braking.

However, my bold venture did not go unnoticed. Upon my return, my father was visibly angry. He made it clear that moving the car was not part of my assigned chores, and he did not appreciate my unauthorized joyride. From that day forward, he took extra precautions, keeping the car keys securely with him and restricting my involvement to washing the exterior only.

Undeterred by my father's admonishment, I found opportunities when he would inadvertently leave the keys within my reach. Each time, I seized the chance to further hone my driving skills, taking the car for short drives around the neighborhood. It became a clandestine operation, a delicate balance between respecting my father's wishes and satisfying my desire to master the skill of driving.

In the absence of formal lessons or guidance, I relied on trial and error. Every drive was a lesson, every mistake an opportunity to refine my technique. I learned the nuances of the clutch's engagement, the optimal moments for gear shifts, and the importance of maintaining awareness in traffic. My self-imposed driving education was a continuous process of improvement and refinement.

Over time, my covert driving sessions evolved into a well-practiced routine. The repetitive nature of washing the car provided me with ample opportunities to sneak in a few minutes behind the wheel. I became attuned to the hum of the engine, the feel of the steering wheel in my hands, and the satisfying click of the gears falling into place.

As weeks turned into months, my confidence behind the wheel grew and I began to venture beyond the familiar streets, exploring the outskirts of our neighborhood. The car, once a daunting piece of machinery, now felt like an extension of myself. The once intimidating manual transmission became second nature, and I no longer had to consciously think about each gear change.

My father, oblivious to my continued clandestine driving lessons, continued to keep a watchful eye on the car keys. However, he gradually relaxed his guard, assuming that my interest in driving had waned. Little did he know that, behind his back, I was becoming a proficient and confident driver.

The turning point came when my father, perhaps

unknowingly, left the keys accessible for the whole day when he went to work in his official police-issued vehicle. Seizing the opportunity, I embarked on a longer drive, navigating through more challenging roads with a newfound sense of mastery. It was during this drive that I realized I had successfully taught myself how to drive.

My self-taught journey was not without its challenges and risks. I had pushed boundaries and navigated the complexities of driving without formal instruction. Yet, in doing so, I gained a valuable skill that would serve me for a lifetime. The independence and self-reliance I developed through this unconventional process became as essential to me as the skill of driving itself.

Looking back, I acknowledge the importance of a structured and supervised learning environment for acquiring driving skills. My self-taught approach was certainly unconventional and not recommended, as it involved risks and could have resulted in serious consequences. I recognize the privilege of emerging unscathed from this experience, but I also appreciate the lessons it imparted – the importance of resilience, adaptability, and the pursuit of knowledge even in the absence of formal guidance.

My journey of teaching myself how to drive was a blend of observation and experimentation. While the circumstances were far from ideal, the experience shaped me in ways that extended beyond the realm of driving. It taught me the value of perseverance, the thrill of independence, and the ability to learn and adapt in unconventional situations. The road I traveled may have been unconventional, but the destination was the same – the acquisition of a valuable life skill and a sense of self-reliance that continues to guide me today.

A Journey Without Wheels: Navigating High School Days in Nigeria

Growing up in Nigeria, the idea of a high school student driving their car to school was as foreign as the distant lands depicted in our geography textbooks. The majority of my classmates and I relied on public transportation, bicycles, or the timeless tradition of walking to and from our boarding houses to class. The notion of cruising to class in a personal vehicle was a distant dream; one that seemed to belong to a reality far removed from the one we inhabited.

Nigeria, with its diverse cultures and traditions, often shapes the way individuals approach life. In my community, the prevailing sentiment was that high school was a time for learning, discipline, and character-building, not for the indulgence of material luxuries like owning a car. Parents, most of whom worked hard to provide their children with a quality education, seldom entertained the idea of gifting their high schoolers with automobiles. The value placed on education eclipsed any desire for extravagant displays of affluence.

My high school experience was further shaped by the fact that I attended a Catholic boarding school. Boarding schools in Nigeria are known for their strict rules and regulations, emphasizing discipline and academic excellence. The environment was structured to foster a sense of community and shared responsibility among students. The idea of having a personal car would have disrupted this carefully crafted ecosystem, giving rise to issues of inequality and a potential distraction from the core focus of education.

Beyond the cultural and institutional reasons, the financial realities of most parents in my school made the prospect of owning a car during high school an impractical fantasy. Nigeria, like many developing nations, faces economic challenges that affect the majority of its population. While aspirations for progress and success are universal, the means to achieve them are not always readily available. In the context of my high school, the notion of parents affording cars for their children was a luxury reserved for the elite, a reality that remained out of reach for the vast majority.

The absence of cars in my high school experience, however, did not diminish the richness of my journey. Instead, it fostered a strong sense of camaraderie among students as we navigated the challenges of adolescence together. The daily walks to and from school became opportunities for bonding, sharing stories, and forming lasting friendships. Attending a boarding school, though often crowded and occasionally unpredictable, became a shared adventure that added a unique flavor to my high school memories.

The lack of personal vehicles also instilled a sense of independence and resourcefulness in me. I learned to manage my time efficiently and navigate the intricacies of boarding school life. These skills, honed during my high school years, would prove valuable in the years to come as I ventured into the broader world beyond the school gates.

Looking back, the absence of cars in my high school experience seems almost poetic. It reinforced the idea that education was the great equalizer; a pursuit that transcended social and economic disparities. In a society where material possessions often define success, my high school experience taught me that true wealth lies in knowledge, character, and the bonds we forge with our peers.

While the absence of cars in high school was a cultural norm, it also served as a reminder of the broader economic challenges faced by many families in Nigeria. The dream of owning a car, while seemingly trivial in the context of education, reflected a larger societal aspiration for economic prosperity and upward mobility. It highlighted the need for systemic changes that would empower more families to provide their children with not only quality education but also the means to access opportunities beyond the confines of their immediate circumstances.

Me and my "Leggedise Benz" in
Benin City, Bendel State Nigeria

Balancing Act: A Journey Through Soccer, Tennis, and the Struggle for Approval

When I was young, the world seemed to stretch endlessly before me, filled with opportunities to explore and discover my passions. Like many children, I gravitated toward sports, and my early years were marked by the rhythmic cadence of soccer balls on the field and the satisfying smack of a tennis racket meeting the ball. Amidst the multitude of sports that beckoned, soccer and tennis stood out as my primary pursuits. However, my journey was not without its hurdles — both metaphorical and literal.

Soccer, with its dynamic gameplay and the camaraderie of teammates, was my first love. The expansive green field became a canvas for our dreams and aspirations, and I reveled in the thrill of scoring goals and the joy of shared victories. Those early years of chasing after the ball and perfecting my kicks forged enduring memories and friendships. Soccer was not just a game; it was a symphony of youthful energy and exuberance.

Tennis, on the other hand, offered a different kind

of challenge. The solitary nature of the sport appealed to me, and the precision required to navigate the court resonated with my competitive spirit.

It wasn't long before I found myself participating in the 100-meter hurdles and the 100-meter sprint as well, seeking to test the limits of my athleticism. However, my romance with hurdles would be short-lived.

The 100-meter hurdles proved to be a formidable adversary. The rhythmic dance between sprinting and leaping over hurdles became a test of agility and fearlessness. Unfortunately, fear had its grip on me, and my attempts often resulted in collisions with the unforgiving barriers. The sharp sting of hitting my legs on those hurdles left a lasting impression, and the fear of injury became a shadow that loomed over my every attempt. Despite the allure of the challenge, I made the difficult decision to step away from the hurdles, recognizing that my safety and well-being were paramount.

In contrast, tennis became my refuge, a haven where my skills could flourish without the specter of potential harm. I dedicated myself to the sport, honing my technique and strategy on the court. My efforts bore fruit when I earned the opportunity to represent my school in the junior division tennis championship at the state tournament. The thrill of competition, the satisfying thud of a well-executed serve, and the elation of victory fueled my passion for tennis.

However, my growing success in tennis became a source of contention with my father. Despite my ability to balance both academics and sports, he disapproved of my commitment to tennis. In his eyes, the hours spent on the court were hours that should have been devoted to textbooks and study sessions. The clash between my father's expectations and my desire to pursue my passion created a tension that lingered beneath the surface of my athletic achievements.

The struggle for parental approval became a formidable opponent, eclipsing the challenges presented by any opponent on the soccer field or tennis court. It wasn't that my father lacked appreciation for the discipline and dedication sports instilled; rather, he feared that my focus on athletics would detract from my academic pursuits. As I continued to excel in tennis, the gap between his expectations and my aspirations widened.

The combination of my father's disapproval and my love for tennis created a paradox that I grappled with throughout my formative years. On one hand, I was determined to prove that excellence in sports and academics could coexist harmoniously. On the other, the desire for parental approval lingered as a persistent undercurrent, shaping my decisions, and influencing the trajectory of my athletic journey. As I reflect on those years, I recognize the importance of striking a balance between passion and pragmatism. While my love for tennis fueled my determination to overcome obstacles, the lessons learned on the field extended beyond the boundaries of sportsmanship. Discipline, time management, and resilience became my allies, helping me navigate the intricate dance between academia and athletics.

In the end, I did not manage to find a middle ground on the issue with my dad, so my tennis-playing days came to an end. Today, as I look back on the soccer fields, and tennis courts, and the hurdles I faced, I recognize the intricate interplay between passion and practicality. The pursuits of my youth, once seen as opposing paths, converged into a narrative of personal growth and resilience. The scars from the collisions with hurdles, both physical and metaphorical, serve as reminders of the challenges overcome and the strength gained through adversity.

The journey from the soccer fields to the tennis courts wasn't just a physical transition; it was a metaphorical exploration of identity, ambition, and the pursuit of happiness. It taught me that the pursuit of one's passions, even in the face of disapproval, is a testament to individuality and the courage to forge one's path. The story of my youth is a mosaic of experiences, with soccer and tennis as the vibrant tiles that form the tapestry of my early years—a tapestry woven with the threads of ambition, resilience, and the pursuit of self-discovery.

Navigating Differences: A Journey of Faith and Education

Growing up in Nigeria, my relationship with my parents, particularly my father, was shaped by the convergence and divergence of our beliefs and aspirations. Two significant areas of contention emerged during my formative years: my departure from the Catholic Church to embrace a non-denominational faith and my decision to pursue higher education in the United States. These choices became pivotal points in my life, sparking intense discussions and challenging the deeply ingrained values that shaped my family.

Leaving the Catholic Church marked a profound shift in the dynamics of my relationship with my father. In Nigeria, where religion often serves as a cornerstone of cultural identity, the Catholic Church was more than a place of worship—it was a symbol of tradition, heritage, and social cohesion. My decision to stop attending the Catholic Church and explore a non-denominational congregation was personal and was met with resistance, especially from my father, who viewed my departure as a betrayal of the Christian faith as he understood it.

The Catholic faith has been an integral part of our

family for generations. Sundays were sacred, filled with the rituals of attending Mass, partaking in the sacraments, and engaging in community events. The prospect of breaking away from this tightly woven fabric of tradition was daunting. However, as I grew older, I found myself questioning certain aspects of Catholic doctrine and seeking a more personal connection with spirituality.

The non-denominational church I chose to attend provided a different approach to faith — one that emphasized a direct and personal relationship with God, free from the elaborate rituals and structures that characterized Catholicism. This shift was met with skepticism and disapproval from my father, who saw my departure as a rejection of our shared values. Nevertheless, it marked the beginning of a spiritual journey that allowed me to forge a deeper connection with my beliefs.

Despite the tension, I sought to communicate the sincerity of my spiritual exploration, emphasizing the universal aspects of faith that transcended denominational boundaries.

However, bridging this ideological gap proved to be a challenging endeavor. Another significant point of contention arose when I expressed my desire to pursue higher education in the United States. In Nigeria, the importance of education is indisputable, but the idea of leaving the familiar confines of home for a foreign land was met with both concern and resistance. My father, deeply rooted in the traditions of our community, found it difficult to comprehend why I would willingly choose to leave the comfort of our home and community and embark on a journey thousands of miles away to a place where I knew no one.

For my father, the decision to leave Nigeria was more than a pursuit of knowledge; it was a departure from the established order of things. While education was highly valued, and the fact that I am the first son, it was expected of me to obtain my higher education within the boundaries of our homeland.

The disagreements with my father over my departure from the Catholic Church and my decision to leave Nigeria were not easy to navigate. These disagreements tested both of our patience and I was not giving up since I believed that my steps were been guided by God's plan for my life and that it was solely a personal choice.

One of the most challenging aspects of our disagreements was the clash of generational values. My father's strong attachment to tradition and cultural heritage was deeply ingrained, shaped by decades of social and religious conditioning. On the other hand, my choices were reflective of a newer generation seeking individuality, personal fulfillment, and a broader understanding of the world.

In the case of my departure from the Catholic Church, I had to communicate that my decision was not an outright rejection of our shared values but rather a personal exploration of faith. It was an attempt to find a spiritual path that resonated more deeply with my beliefs and allowed for a more personal connection with God. This required patience and understanding on both sides, as we navigated the delicate balance between honoring tradition and embracing individual growth. However, my father never saw it that way and believed that he should make the final decision regarding my personal faith, and this caused a lot of distance between us.

Similarly, when it came to leaving Nigeria for

education, I had to convey that my decision was driven by a quest for knowledge and personal development. It was not a disregard for the rich culture of Nigeria but my recognition of the voice inside of me that I can no longer ignore. I also realized that my father's resistance and decision have been influenced by his cousins and my uncle who were against my leaving Nigeria to further my education.

For me, the experience of standing firm in my decisions, even in the face of family disapproval, fostered a sense of independence and self-discovery. It taught me the importance of pursuing a path that aligns with my values and aspirations, even when it diverges from the expectations of those closest to me. Over time, as I continued to attend the non-denominational church and pursued my education in the United States, my father began to acknowledge the validity of my choices.

The journey of disagreeing with my parents, particularly my father, on matters as significant as religious faith and educational pursuits, was challenging yet transformative. It required navigating the delicate balance between honoring tradition and embracing personal growth, and it demanded resilience and open communication. Through these disagreements, I learned the importance of staying true to my convictions while also seeking to understand and respect the perspectives of others.

The experience taught me that disagreements within families are not merely conflicts to be overcome but opportunities for growth and understanding. It underscored the idea that diverging from established norms, whether in matters of faith or life choices, can lead to a deeper understanding of oneself and those we love.

Crossing Borders: The Decision to Come to the United States

After I completed my high school final exams, I found myself walking around the campus and taking in the memories of high school when I came across one of my classmates. To this day, I cannot remember his name. However, while we were talking, I asked him about his plans after high school and he said he was going to join the Blue Devils.

"The Blue Devils?" I asked.

He said, "Yes, I am going to the Blue Devils."

I further inquired what the Blue Devils were. He showed me a package with the imprint of Dillard University's Blue Devils. It was the mascot for Dillard University in New Orleans. He then proceeded to give me one of the application packages. "You can have one," he said, "I have two."

I said, "Okay, I will hold onto it." I had no plans to use it because I planned to attend either University of Lagos, the University of Ibadan, or the University of Ife, which were all in Nigeria. I wanted to study medicine in Nigeria and studying abroad was not part of my plan.

A few weeks after graduating from high school, I

went to visit one of my aunties. While at her home, my cousin decided to visit one of his friends who lived across the street. He asked me to come along. We then visited his friend; there were two other people there and he introduced me to them. About an hour into our visit, one of his friends told us they were about to go to the passport office to see one of his older brother's friends who worked there. The guy wanted to apply and obtain an international passport. He asked us to accompany him to the office. My cousin could not go, however, his friend turned to me and said, "You better come with us because one day, if you plan to go to the United States, you will need a passport so let me show you the process." I agreed and followed them to the Passport Office.

On our way there, I asked why they needed an international passport and he said he would be going to the United States to further his education at Texas Southern University in Houston, Texas. He had already gotten admission to study at the school but he now needed to obtain an international passport so he could travel.

Neither one of us had money to take the bus so we walked about 8 miles to the passport office. Upon our arrival, we met his older brother's friend. He gave us the passport application to fill out and told us to get our passport picture taken at Ring Road (that was the closest place to take and get an instant passport picture) and return with it.

When we arrived at the place to get our picture taken, we were told it would take two hours for the passport pictures to be ready and it would cost N20 (Twenty Naira) an equivalent of $15 at that time for a set of four passport pictures each. I told my cousin's friend that I did not have any money to pay my share of the passport pictures or the international passport application fee of N20 (Twenty Naira). He then used the office phone to call his brother and explained the situation to him and after his phone conversation with his brother, he told us that his brother would help with the money we needed. We then walked to his brother's office. When we got to the office, he introduced us to his brother, and without any question, his brother gave him the money the three of us needed for the passport pictures and application fee. In addition, he gave us money for transportation and to buy food since we had not eaten all day.

We retraced our steps to the photography studio to have our passport pictures taken, and then we headed back to the passport office. There, we handed over the passport photos, the duly completed international passport application, and the requisite fees to his brother's friend. Taking charge, he went to converse with his supervisors, vouching for us as his friends in need of international passports for travel. After a brief thirty-minute wait, we were handed our passports. And just like that, I acquired my first international passport.

It was a remarkably interesting day because that was the first time I met my cousin's friend, Kenneth Iduwonyi. He treated me as if we had known each other for a long time and Kenneth was only one year older than me. I was a little reserved and skeptical but, by the end of the day, we had become friends.

On our way home, Kenneth said he needed to go to the courthouse in the Secretariat building the next day to see his brother. He needed to get some money to get several documents notarized. These were part of the documents required, in addition to, his international passport to go to the United States Embassy in Lagos for a visa. He asked if I could go with him. I said, "no problem." We met the next day, and I followed him around observing all the steps required to apply for the student visa. He said it's very possible one day I may decide that I want to go to the United States to study. Now I knew how to undergo the process myself.

During the process, I listened to Kenneth and observed. We first went to the courthouse to get the required affidavits notarized. From there, we went to the Ministry of Education to get the approvals required by the US Embassy Visa Office. Afterward, we proceeded to obtain documents from the Health Department, and Kenneth got his required International Immunization Health Card from the clinic on Airport Road in Benin. His final step in the process was the interview at the US Embassy in Lagos to obtain a student visa. He interviewed and was issued a four-year visa to study at Texas Southern University in Houston, Texas. I was very happy for him. Shortly after receiving his student visa, his older brother purchased his plane ticket, and he traveled out of Nigeria as he had planned.

When Kenneth Iduwonyi left Benin City for the United States, I started thinking about the possibility of doing the same. My main obstacle was my dad. He would not approve, and I also thought it was out of my reach.

I knew that if I got a good university education when I graduated, I would be able to get an excellent job and live a comfortable life. As I stated earlier, I wanted to attend either the University of Lagos, the University of Ibadan, or the University of Ife. My dad insisted that I attend the University of Benin because it was in the same city we lived. I found this ironic because throughout my high school education, my dad had me attending schools in rural areas and cities outside of Benin City. I wanted to attend high school in Benin City, yet he did everything in his power to make sure that I attended high school outside of Benin City. Now, I wanted to get away from Benin City and he was insisting that I must attend university in Benin City to be close to home. Wonders never cease.

Not wanting to draw much attention to myself while I was considering going to the US to study, I kept it to myself. I knew my dad would be furious. I wanted time to think and plan my next step. I went into my closet and retrieved the Dillard University application package that was given to me by my high school classmate, which I had tucked away for over a year and a half.

After a few weeks, I told my mother that I wanted to go to school in the United States of America. Her reply was, "You better tell your father and I foresee this is going to be a big problem." When my dad returned home from work, I told him that I wanted to go to school in the United States. He was furious and gave me every reason in the world why I would not be going. He stated that I would be attending the University of Benin in Nigeria. I figured if I gained admission to a school in the United States, and then approached my dad once again with an admission letter, he would change his mind.

I went ahead and completed the Dillard University application for admission, as well as a Texas Southern University application that I had obtained from my friend, Kenneth Iduwonyi. My problem was that I had no financial means to get the international bank draft in dollars needed for the application fees. I asked my mother for help, and she suggested that I go see my uncle. My father's first cousin, John Airiohuodion was a regional manager at Barclays Bank (now Union Bank). I went to see him at his office on Mission Road in Benin City.

I knew it was going to be tough dealing with my uncle because he was not a very nice man. I went to my uncle's office as my mother had suggested and told him that I needed two bank drafts; one for about $7 and the other for $12 to pay for the application fees for US schools. He looked at me and told me to wait outside his office until he called me back in to discuss further.

I waited outside his office from 9:00 am to 3:00 pm. He never asked me to come back into his office. After waiting for such a long time, I finally asked his assistant if he could remind my uncle that I was still waiting for him. The assistant came back and said my uncle knew that I was still outside his office waiting. At 4:30 pm I asked my uncle's assistant again. He told me that my uncle left for the day.

Surprised, I asked, "Did you tell him I was still waiting for him?" He responded that my uncle used the private back exit door and told him to let me know if I made another inquiry that he should tell me to come back the next day. I waited all day with no water or food and watched other people walk in and out of his office.

Since I had no other means of getting the bank drafts, I decided that I would try again the next day. So, the next day I went back to see him. His assistant went and told my uncle I was back in the office. He told me to wait outside again. While I was waiting outside, one of my aunties, Mama Ehiemua walked into the bank and noticed that I was sitting outside my uncle's office. She asked if my uncle was not in the office. I told her what had happened the previous day and my reason for sitting outside waiting again. She then told me to come with her. She marched into my uncle's office and demanded why he kept me outside waiting and why he left the bank the previous day without attending to me. She was furious with him and demanded an answer from him. He started trying to calm Mama Ehiemua down. She then told my uncle that he must not treat family members in this despicable manner.

My uncle then asked me what I wanted. I said my mother told me to come to see him process two bank drafts to pay for US university application fees. I will never forget what my uncle said to me that day. He said "Mark, you are a useless son. You just want to go to America to waste your father's money. Why would you want to go to school in America when you could go to school in Nigeria? The only people who went to school in America were those who failed high school and were not good enough to get into Nigerian universities. You passed your high school exams and you must attend the University of Benin."

It was at that moment I realized that he had spoken to my dad concerning his insistence that I attend the University of Benin. My aunt told him that he was lying because one of her sons, very smart, went to school in Houston, Texas, and still lives in Texas.

My uncle continued ranting saying, "Mark passed his high school exams and gained admission into Nigerian universities, but he is choosing not to go because he is a useless son!" He continued saying that I was going to waste my time and my father's money. My auntie was furious and chastised him never to say things like that again about his cousin's son. He then told my Aunty that he would process the bank drafts for me and asked me to sit down in his office so he could attend to my Aunty. About fifteen minutes later my Aunty left his office. He then turned his attention to me and said that he would not give me the bank drafts and ordered me to leave his office and never to return. He got up and left the office for the day.

When I got home, I told my mother what my uncle said and did, and she said, "I will talk to your father about it." When my dad got home from work, my mother called me to the living room and told my dad what his cousin did. My dad said he did not believe any of it because his cousin called him before leaving his office that I came to his workplace, insulted him, and had my aunt join in insulting him as well.

I had no idea how I was going to be able to get the bank draft to pay the application fee. I prayed for God to help me since I didn't know any other person or banker who would be able to help me. I continued to pray that God would send someone my way to help me since my dad was not interested in helping my effort. If he wanted, he could have made a phone call and had the bank drafts delivered to him at home.

One evening my friend Tony and I were sitting by the stairway at our house. My father's tenant, Mr. Igueze, who lived downstairs below the flat we lived in heard my conversation with Tony concerning my uncle's horrible treatment of me at his bank. He called me the next morning and said that he had overheard my conversation with Tony, and he asked me if I knew what he does for a living. I answered, "No sir." I knew he worked in an office but nothing specific and his wife was a school teacher.

He told me that he was an accountant at the New

Nigerian Bank. He asked me how much was the bank draft that I needed. I responded one for US$7 and the second one for US$12 and I explained to him what happened between my uncle and me. He said not to worry and come by his office the next day that he will have the bank drafts ready for me. I further explained to him that I did not have any money to pay for the bank draft. His response was do not worry about that, just come, and pick up the drafts. I then gave him the names of the universities and the amount for each school to issue the draft.

The next day, I went to his office and as promised, he handed me the bank drafts; one made out to Dillard University and the other made out to Texas Southern University. I inserted the drafts in my ready-to-mail application packages and went to the post office to mail them off. Within two months, I received an admission letter from Dillard University in New Orleans, Louisiana.

Upon receiving the letter of admission, I started thinking about how I was going to pay my school fees since my dad had refused to listen to anything that did not involve attending the University of Benin. How would I pay for the visa-required affidavits, Ministry of Education, and health documents needed by the US Embassy? How would I pay for my travel ticket to the United States? Who was going to help me? These were all the questions in my head. Above all, I did not know anyone in the United States. I knew that I must follow the steps that I had learned from my friend Kenneth before he departed for the United States.

I believe to this day that the way I met Kenneth Iduwonyi was not coincidental but ordained by God. Without the means and the support from my dad, my plans to travel to the United States were going to be difficult. I began to feel sad because I saw my friend Kenneth go through the process, but he had his older brother's support. I knew that my situation was different.

I continued to pray for God's guidance and at one point my spirit was troubled. I knew that God was making a way for me to leave Nigeria by allowing me to meet Kenneth and witness the process firsthand. Once I was convinced that God was steering my course, my mind was made up and there was no turning back. I was fully convinced that God had put the idea of leaving Nigeria in my heart. All I needed to do was to look at how everything was unfolding. God has always been in the mix.

I told my mother that I must continue this path of traveling to the US to continue my education. I needed her help in securing funds to pay for documents. She gave me some money and I retraced the steps that I had observed my friend Kenneth follow. I knew what to do, where to go, and whom to talk to. I started the process and got all my documents together by going to the courthouse for the affidavits, the Ministry of Education for the required documents, and the Ministry of Health for my international immunization.

Due to my dad's refusal to assist me in the process, I went to one of my mother's older brothers, Judge Michael Ojo, who was a federal judge to talk to my dad on my behalf. I also went to one of my dad's good friends, Mr. Olaikere, who was the principal at Asaba Technical College to talk to my dad. They both tried to convince my dad to allow me to travel to the United States for college.

My dad now realized that I was not letting go of the idea of going to America. One day he was walking up the stairs after work, and my friend Tony and I were sitting on the staircase as usual. My dad stopped and offered me N40 naira to get an international passport. I thanked him and told him I did not need the passport money because I already had an international passport. His surprised expression was priceless when I told him that I had an international passport!

With my letter of admission from Dillard University and all the required documents, I was ready to go to Lagos for a visa interview at the United States Embassy. I went to my uncle Judge Ojo's house in Lagos, and he dropped me off at the US Embassy on Victoria Island early the next morning for my interview. The US Embassy was crowded. There was a long line of visa applicants wrapped around the corner before the Embassy was opened for business.

When the Embassy opened, we were ushered into a sitting area where we waited until our name was called to the window. While I was waiting, several names were called, and all the applicants were denied a visa. It was evident by the expressions on their faces. When my name was finally called to the window for an interview, I was totally at peace with whatever the outcome. I felt that I had done everything within my power and prayed silently that God's will be done.

The gentleman conducting the interview asked me why I wanted to go to the United States, and I told him to study. He asked me why not in Nigeria. I said I needed to get out of Nigeria to study. He then asked for my passport, and I gave it to him. All the prepared documents from the Ministry of Education, and affidavits from the Ministry of Health that I brought with me in sealed envelopes were never requested from me.

He only asked to see my admission documents from Dillard University, and I gave it to him. He then continued staring straight into my eyes for a few minutes which seemed like an hour. He then asked me to go back and sit down. After about two hours, he called my name to come back to the window. I did and he looked me in the eyes and said, "Welcome to the United States of America, and good luck!" He handed me my passport with a four-year student visa stamped on it.

I had just turned 18 years old two months prior, and I was about to embark on the adventure of a lifetime. I did not even know where the United States was on the world map.

I hated geography while in high school and now I had a four-year student visa in my international passport to study in the United States of America. Unbelievable! I was so excited. With my passport in my pocket, I left Lagos for Benin that same day.

I know if not for the grace of God I would have never gotten that visa. In reflection, I believe it was in God's grand plan for me to be where I am today. To leave Nigeria for the United States to study at Dillard University in New Orleans.

When I arrived home in Benin City, my mother was sitting upstairs on the outside patio area looking worried. I greeted her and walked inside the house straight to my room. She followed me to my room with a worried look on her face. "So how did it go?" She asked.

I told my her I got a four-year student visa to study in the United States. I then showed her the visa stamp on my passport. She looked at me with shock, not believing the possibility. I replied, "Yes, I got it and all I need now is a plane ticket!"

She just stared at me in shock. I guess she was prepared for the worst – me not getting a visa. The next day my mother told my dad that I had a visa to go study in the United States. My dad responded that no one would give me a visa and that he was not going to be involved in that conversation because there are schools in Nigeria for me to attend.

A few days later my mother asked me if I was going to the United States I replied yes, and the only thing that I needed now was a plane ticket. Furthermore, I told her that when I got to America, I would work as hard as I could to pay for school and nothing or no one was going to stop me.

That evening when my dad was watching the evening news on television, she told my dad that he needed to talk with me because I was getting ready to leave Benin City and go to the United States. She warned him that if you let him go with the way things are between both of you, Mark would never speak to you again. The next day he asked to see my admission letter from Dillard University. I gave him a copy of the original fearing he would tear it up. He asked to see the visa in my passport, and I showed it to him from a distance fearing he would rip my passport in two.

About a week after getting my student visa, my dad came home from work; he gave me bank drafts for one-year school fees and traveler's checks. He said since I decided to study outside Nigeria, he would not be sending me any more money. If circumstances get too difficult in America, I am on my own and should rough it or I can come back home and attend one of the universities in Nigeria. I decided then that failure was not an option.

This is Lawrence Osaigbovo and me. He was one of my dear friends. Lawrence was an officer in the Nigerian Customs Service in Lagos. If I had not made the decision to come to the United States to study, I was going to enlist into the Customs Service. Lawrence rose to the position of Deputy Director of Customs before passing in an automobile accident.

Dillard University's Basketball team logo

Leaving Home:
Embracing the Unknown

Upon obtaining my student visa, the realization dawned that securing a plane ticket marked the next step toward my journey to the United States — a day eagerly anticipated in my life. This juncture brought forth a mix of emotions, as I felt both joy for the impending adventure and sadness at the prospect of parting with my parents, siblings, and other cherished family and friends. Stepping into an unknown future, in a different world with distinct cultures and unfamiliar faces, raised uncertainties about whether my background and way of life would be understood or appreciated.

Amidst these concerns, I held onto the belief that God accompanied me on this transformative journey. The idea of traveling to the United States was divinely planted in my heart, signifying a grand plan that I was prepared to embrace, regardless of the challenges it might present. Central to this plan was the unwavering commitment to pursue my education, the primary motivation for leaving Nigeria.

As I departed Nigeria for the U.S., my mind was a swirl of contemplated scenarios. "What ifs" dominated my thoughts — what if the reality differed from my expectations, what if it proved to be a hazardous place, what if I struggled to adapt, what if my dreams remained unfulfilled, and what if my decision to embark on this journey was a mistake? Resolute, I resolved to accept the consequences of my choice, emphasizing the need to trust in God's overarching plan and maintaining faith in my ability to overcome challenges.

The departure day was marked by poignant moments with my siblings, uncles, aunties, and friends, who gathered at our house for pictures. Some accompanied me to the local airport in Benin, extending heartfelt farewells. The gravity of the situation sank in as I left Benin City, bound for Lagos, where I would board a plane to the United States. The departure date, August 18, 1982, solidified the significance of this chapter in my life.

Lawrence Osaigbovo and I the day I left Benin City
to travel to the United States. August 18, 1982

My brother Ken and I on the day I left Benin City

Journey to a New Beginning: Arrival in a Foreign Land

My journey to the United States was long and tiring. The flight was four segments with me leaving from Benin Airport.

First, I boarded a Nigerian Airways flight from Benin City to Lagos. The flight was only about 45 minutes after takeoff. The plane landed at the local airport in Ikeja, Lagos. I took a taxi to the International Airport which was just a twenty minute drive due to heavy traffic. When I arrived at the international airport, I had to go through security to enter the airport and proceeded to check in at KLM Royal Dutch Airlines. Then I went through customs and more security before getting to the waiting area to board the long-anticipated flight to the United States with a stopover in Amsterdam, Netherlands.

I had to wait six hours before boarding the flight from Lagos to Amsterdam, which was about ten hours flight time. Upon arriving at the Schiphol International Airport in Amsterdam, I decided to get a room at the Ibis Hotel which was recommended by the KLM desk agents at the airport since my connecting flight was scheduled for the next day. The hotel was a short distance from the airport, and they provided a free shuttle. Most of the passengers who were transiting to the United States also decided to check into the hotel for the night.

When I stepped out of the airport to catch the Ibis Hotel courtesy bus, it was very cold. It was the very first time that I experienced chilly weather like that.

The Ibis Hotel was clean and charming. At the check-in desk were baskets full of red delicious apples. I must say that was the very first time that I saw and ate an apple. I remember walking around the hotel grounds and there were apple trees with red fruits on them and guests were encouraged to pluck an apple off the apple trees anytime they wanted.

The next day, I boarded the hotel courtesy bus back to the airport for the final part of my journey to the United States. It was also an exceptionally long flight of about 18 hours. Airplanes were not as fast as they are now. We finally arrived at JFK International Airport in New York, then I boarded a connecting flight to New Orleans, Louisiana, which was my final destination. The flight from JFK to New Orleans was very short, about 3 hours compared to my other flights. When I finally made it to New Orleans, I was so exhausted! However, I was ready for my new adventure.

Bayou Bound: My First Impressions of New Orleans

I had no real expectations upon my arrival in New Orleans on August 20, 1982. I was tired and anxious to get to Dillard University and get a good night's rest. My flight to New Orleans arrived late in the evening. After picking up my luggage, I proceeded to the exit gate of the airport, and I asked a police officer for assistance in getting a cab to Dillard University telling him that I was from Nigeria, and it was my first time in the United States.

The officer stopped a cab and instructed the driver to take me to Dillard University. He told me that it would only cost $20 for the cab fare and thirty minutes to get there and if the cab driver charged me more the $20, I should contact him. He then handed me his business card. He further told the cab driver that he had his license plate written down. He was an immensely helpful and kind officer. The ride from the airport to Dillard University was only about thirty minutes and cost only $20 just as the officer had said.

I still believe today that Dillard University has
one of the most beautiful campuses.

Stepping Onto a New Path: My Arrival at Dillard University

Upon arriving at Dillard University, I told the gateman, Mr. Miller, my name and that I was a new international student. He checked a login list and made a phone call and asked the driver to proceed and drop me off as close as he could to the male dormitory, Camphor Hall, pointing his finger in the direction of the dormitory.

My first impression of Dillard University was that it was an incredibly beautiful school. I still think that it is one of the most beautiful college campuses in the United States. The huge white buildings were strategically placed around the campus. From Gentilly Blvd., you can see the beauty of the campus with its perfectly manicured lawns and well-kept grounds.

When I arrived at my assigned dorm room, I started reminiscing about my conversation with my old high school classmate who gave me one of his admission application packages referring to Dillard saying that he was going to the United States to study at the Blue Devils about the Dillard University basketball mascot-Dillard Blue Devils.

It was unfortunate that he never came and attended

Dillard University. I am sure he would have loved it. I pray that life has treated him well. Sometimes I wonder how things would have played out if we had not seen each other on that faithful day. I hope life treated him well because if not for our divine meeting that day, I would not have heard about Dillard University at that very critical time in my life. I believe that God in His master plan set up our meeting that day.

Dorm Life Chronicles: My Journey on Dillard University's Campus

Upon my arrival at Dillard University, I was assigned to Camphor Hall where I shared a room on the second floor with Jack Jackson, a fellow student from Chicago, Illinois. Living on campus was not an issue for me and the transition was easy because I attended boarding school when I was in high school. In high school, it was more of a military-style housing where bunk beds were set up in a large hall. So, sharing a room with another student was not a problem.

Living on campus had its benefits such as it was easy to access the classrooms, library, cafeteria, and other social events that took place on campus. The food served on campus was not that good from my point of view but since I did not come to the United States to eat, it did not bother me that much. However, campus politics took on a life of its own. While some of the American students were helpful and welcoming others made life a little difficult and hostile towards African students.

Some of the male American students felt threatened in ways that were hard for me to comprehend. Words like, "Go back to your country; you are just here to take our women, education, and jobs back to Africa" were commonly used against African students on campus. I was very surprised by the behavior of some of the students because they were black students discriminating and treating us with contempt. Being discriminated against by fellow black students was something that I was not prepared for and did not understand at that time. However, some good male American students were very receptive to us the African students and wanted to learn more about the African culture.

This is Camphor Hall where I lived when I first arrived.

Trying to relax by the New Orleans Lakefront

Moving Beyond Campus: Transitioning from Dillard University Housing

My decision to transition from on-campus to off-campus living was primarily driven by financial considerations. The cost associated with residing on campus proved to be higher than that of off-campus alternatives. Recognizing the imperative to secure employment for self-sustainment and to fund my college education, I conducted a thorough assessment of my financial situation.

In light of this evaluation, I discerned that securing accommodation off campus, within reasonable proximity to my educational institution, would result in substantial cost savings and alleviate my financial strain. Conscientiously examining my financial standing, I acknowledged the necessity of obtaining gainful employment to support myself and cover the expenses associated with my college education. This realization prompted a thoughtful review of my living arrangements. I contemplated the prospect of securing a room off campus that would not only be financially viable but also within a manageable distance for daily commuting to school. The envisioned outcome was a reduction in my overall expenditure, contributing to a more sustainable financial framework.

To make an informed decision, I meticulously devised a comprehensive budget, taking into account various aspects of living expenses. This involved a meticulous cost comparison between on-campus and off-campus living arrangements. The objective was to ascertain the financial implications of each option and determine the most pragmatic course of action based on my limited financial resources.

Upon completing the budgetary analysis and cost comparison, it became evident that, given my financial constraints, opting for off-campus living was the more judicious choice. The potential savings and reduced financial burden associated with off-campus accommodation outweighed the convenience of on-campus living. This decision was rooted in a strategic approach to managing my financial resources and ensuring a sustainable lifestyle throughout my college tenure.

The process of transitioning from on-campus to off-campus living involved a thoughtful consideration of not only immediate financial implications but also the long-term financial sustainability of my chosen arrangement. It underscored the importance of aligning my living choices with my financial capacity, thereby establishing a foundation for responsible financial management during my college years.

The decision to move off campus was driven by a pragmatic assessment of financial considerations. The recognition of the need for financial stability, coupled with a conscientious evaluation of living expenses, led to the conclusion that off-campus living was a more financially viable option. It was also underpinned by meticulous budgetary analysis and comprehensive cost comparison, ultimately guiding me toward a sustainable and responsible approach to managing my finances while pursuing higher education.

My First Apartment Adventure

After deciding to reduce my financial burden, I started looking for a place off campus. I met other Nigerian students living in an apartment complex not too far away from the Dillard University campus. I then visited the apartment complex where most of them lived and inquired if there was a vacant apartment available or if it would become available soon. Fortunately, I was told that one apartment was available if I could pay the cost of the furniture and assume the rent from the current tenant, a Ghanaian student (Yebuwa) who was moving to Atlanta, Georgia. I eventually met with him, and he offered me the apartment if I could assume the rent of $125 per month and pay him $300 for the furniture he would be leaving behind.

I decided I was going to take the apartment; however, I knew that I could not afford that apartment on my own for a long period and needed someone to share the cost. When I returned to campus, I talked to a couple of other Nigerian students who were looking to move off campus. I inquired if they were willing to share the apartment with me. They agreed to share the apartment but were unwilling to pay for the furniture.

We then made a deal that I would pay for the

furniture and the apartment was mine and they were welcome to move in with me with the understanding that they were just subleasing and would pay their portion of the rent and utilities when due. We also agreed that they could move out as soon as they got their apartment. With all that agreed upon, I moved into the apartment and Remy Odemegu and Charles Nwanbuzor moved in with me a few weeks later.

It was a small one-bedroom apartment with a kitchen, living room, bedroom, and bathroom. The railroad tracks were behind the building and the place shook every time the train passed. There was no shower head in the bathroom so we had to use a bucket to collect water so we could take a shower. There was no heat to warm the place during the winter; I had to turn on the gas oven. I had a small window unit air conditioner; I used a fan to cool the rest of the apartment.

As a student, the apartment was well-fitted for what I needed at that time for the price. Several Nigerian students were attending Dillard University, University of New Orleans, and Southern University who also lived in the complex. A few other tenants that were non-Nigerian also lived there.

The monthly rent was $125. The landlord, Mr. Cordoba, was a very good man. He did not frustrate his tenants; especially the students due to our inability to pay the rent on time. He knew it was difficult for us to work full-time and attend school full-time to meet our obligations. He cut us a lot of slack. His goodness towards us allowed most of us to work very hard to meet our rental obligation to him while completing our education.

A few months later, Charles moved to Chicago and

Remy also moved into his own apartment. Subsequently, I was in the apartment by myself. It was a struggle to pay the rent and my school fees after they both moved out.

In addition to working 12 hours during the weekdays and 16 hours during the weekends as a security guard at night, I started driving a taxicab in between to enable me to earn enough money to pay my tuition and other living expenses. I was determined to complete my education at Dillard University, so I worked long hours with little rest to fulfill my goals.

I really liked this warm-up suit!

"The Embassy"

What was "The Embassy?" The Embassy was a place where love was shared regardless of one's nationality. A place where Africans as well as Americans lived in peace and learned each other's culture. When new African students arrived in New Orleans to study and did not know anyone, cab drivers would let them know that Africans were living in an apartment not too far from Dillard University and the cab drivers or other students would bring them to the 2300 N. Broad apartments.

This is the parking lot at "The Embassy" where we would congregate and socialize on Friday nights. We sure had some great times!

The apartments at 2300 N. Broad housed a lot of Africans, especially Nigerians. It was a home away from home for most Africans who lived there in the 70s, 80s, and 90s. Nigerians, Ghanaians, Cameroonians, and American students met at 2300 N. Broad on Fridays and Saturday evenings for a get-together and reminisce about home and our lives in America trying to make it while going to school and working full time to pay for college. It was not an easy task to do but being around people with similar struggles made the struggle a little easier.

African students who moved from Grambling, Lafayette, and Baton Rouge to New Orleans seemed to find their way to the Embassy as well. After graduating from college, most of us who lived at 2300 N. Broad started moving and seeking better living arrangements in other parts of the city. However, during my college days, it was the place to be.

On Fridays, after school when we were off from work, or before going to work at night, we would all gather in the parking lot playing music, drinking beer or liquor, shooting the breeze, and having a wonderful time. That was how some of our days went and it all happened at 2300 N. Broad Apartments. We sometimes called it "The Embassy" due to the diversity of people who lived there and the camaraderie we shared.

In my
apartment
at the
Embassy,
Spring
1983

The courtyard of "The Embassy." My apartment was on the top left; Clement Osunde's apartment was below mine to the left and Sunny Omofonwan was on the bottom right next to Clement

New Connections: Building Friendships at "The Embassy"

After moving into my apartment on 2300 North Broad (The Embassy). I lived in apartment thirty-three. My next-door neighbor was another Nigerian who was in his final year of accounting at Dillard University. His name was Geoffrey Ekuke but, we called him O'sharee which signifies the greetings from his hometown of the Delta region in Nigeria.

The summer he graduated from Dillard University, he went back home to visit his parents and was killed in a car accident. Communication was not like it is today where everything happens fast. We were notified a few months after the accident occurred. We were all wondering why Geoffrey had not returned. His death was tragic and affected the Nigerian community especially those of us that lived at the Embassy. I believe Geoffrey was one of the first friends that I made at the Embassy. May his soul continue to rest in peace. O'sharee!

Other Nigerians living at the Embassy at that time were very friendly with each other however, in addition to Geoffrey, Sunny Omofonwan, Clement Osunde, and Sonnie Oguigo were the other three people that were the first friends that I made at the Embassy. Sunny was very generous to everyone. He was older, having graduated, and was working. He used to cook soup and rice and share it with us all. We never had to worry about hunger with Sunny around.

Now my friend Clement Osunde was a very jolly fellow. Every time that gray Monte Carlo (we called it "Monte Quey-Quey") pulled into the parking lot at the Embassy, we knew everything was about to break loose! Clement was always the center of attention (in a good way). At our Friday get-together, we would all "broke nose" and have fun. Those were some of my best memories.

To this day we remain friends and visit each other despite living in different states and reminisce about the old days.

Geoffrey Ekuke aka "O'sharee"

O'sharee and I

Sunny and I on a Royal Caribbean cruise - February 2023.

Clement and I in Galveston, Texas, April 2022.

"The Embassy" Shenanigans

I have good memories of living at the Embassy. Every Friday evening after school and before we all had to go to our respective jobs, we got together at the apartment parking lot and had our brand of happy hour. We would eat, drink, and dance to our local music. Mostly, we drank and reminisced about home and our mission in the United States which was to get a good education. We reminded ourselves never to forget the reason we came to the United States and that the hardships we are currently facing would not last forever if we stayed focused. We understood it was not going to be easy, but we also understood that a good, educated person has a better chance of succeeding. Some of us stayed the course, some dropped out of school and others felt the hardship was not worth it and decided to go back home to Nigeria.

The biggest problem was the fact that the majority of us did not have the proper work permit and for those that did, the long hours of working as a security guard at night and going to school full-time were hectic. The Friday social gave us an outlet to vent and drink away our troubles and live to fight another day. I must say those were challenging times because the struggle was real. It wasn't all bad times; we did have a lot of fun on those Friday nights.

On one of those Friday evening gatherings, one of my friends, Reuben, got into an argument with another friend and suddenly he jumped on top of my car to make his point during their argument. I had a red and gray Dodge Challenger at the time. My car had a clear, tempered glass sunroof and as he was standing on the roof, I told him to get down from the top of my car, and he could make his point known while standing on the ground. He ignored me and kept jumping on the car all while holding his liquor in his hand.

Suddenly, the sunroof glass caved in, and he went straight through the broken glass into my car. Amazingly when he landed, he still had a tight grip on the glass. Not one drop had spilled! He just kept apologizing. After realizing he was not injured, we all fell out laughing! I would say that was one of the funniest memories that I had living at the Embassy. To this day he swears that he does not remember what made him climb to the top of my car while arguing with another person.

My 1982 Dodge Challenger

A Culinary Connection: My Unforgettable Encounter with Prince

The transition to a university can be both exhilarating and challenging, marked by the excitement of new friendships and the unfamiliarity of a different environment. My experience at Dillard University took an unexpected turn when my dissatisfaction with cafeteria food led to an encounter with Prince, a fellow Nigerian student. This unanticipated meeting not only satisfied my cravings for home (eating cooked Nigerian cuisine) but also blossomed into a lasting friendship that has spanned forty-plus years.

It all began on a typical Saturday morning when, dissatisfied with the cafeteria offerings, my friends Charles, Remi, and I decided to venture beyond the confines of Dillard University in search of more palatable fare. Our destination was the McDonald's on Gentilly Boulevard. Little did we know that this routine outing would lead to an extraordinary connection.

As we walked towards our destination, a silver Camaro with a distinctive "Playboy" tag pulled up beside us. To our surprise, the driver rolled down his window and inquired if we were new Nigerian students at Dillard.

Affirmative nods were exchanged, and inquisitive gazes met the friendly face of the man behind the wheel. This stranger, as it turned out, was Prince, a fellow Nigerian student at Dillard University.

In the course of our brief conversation, Prince's warmth and hospitality became apparent. Learning about our quest for better food, he extended an invitation that would alter the course of our day. "Why go to McDonald's when you can experience a taste of home?" he proposed, urging us to abandon our fast-food plans in favor of a home-cooked Nigerian meal at his apartment. Intrigued and hungry for a genuine taste of home, we gladly accepted his invitation and hopped into his silver Camaro.

Upon arriving at Prince's apartment, we were greeted by the inviting aroma of spices and the sound of sizzling pots. Prince, it seemed, was not only a welcoming host but also a good cook (I finally said it). He served us rice and stew, Okazi soup, and fufu. It was a culinary journey that transported us back to the tastes of our homeland, a comfort so rare in a foreign land.

As we savored each bite, the conversation flowed effortlessly. Prince shared anecdotes of his own university experience and life in the United States, creating an atmosphere that felt like a reunion with long-lost friends. The barriers that often accompany new friendships dissolved in the warmth of shared cultural experiences and the joy of discovering common ground.

Little did we know that this chance encounter would evolve into a deep and enduring friendship. Prince and I, bound by the threads of shared laughter and cultural affinity, became inseparable. Over the years, we celebrated each other's milestones, with Prince standing by my side as the best man at my wedding and reciprocating the gesture when he tied the knot. Our friendship weathered the challenges of time and distance, proving that the initial spark ignited on that fateful day outside of the Dillard University campus endured.

As the years unfolded, Prince relocated to Richardson, a suburb of Dallas, yet the distance did not dampen the flames of our friendship. We continued to stay connected, bridging the geographical gap through phone calls, video chats, and occasional visits. The bond formed over a shared love of Nigerian cuisine and a mutual journey through university life had transcended the confines of a campus, transforming into a lifelong connection.

My encounter with Prince at Dillard University remains etched in my memory as a testament to the unpredictable beauty of life's twists and turns. What began as a quest for a satisfying meal led to the discovery of a friend whose impact on my life transcends the boundaries of time and space. Through shared laughter, cultural connections, and the aroma of home-cooked meals, Prince became more than a friend – he became a brother. Our journey from strangers to lifelong friends exemplifies the transformative power of unexpected connections, proving that sometimes, the most meaningful relationships blossom from the most ordinary moments.

Prince and I are in Richardson, Texas.

Prince, at my apartment on Crowder Blvd in the 80s.

My First Year at Dillard University

My journey at Dillard University marked the beginning of a chapter filled with both excitement and apprehension as I embarked on the academic challenges of university life. Settling into the dormitory, I was eager to immerse myself in the learning environment, but a sense of anxiety lingered as I contemplated the demands of university-level classes. Among my initial courses was English 101; a class taught by Mr. Smith, a proficient instructor with an intriguing twist to his personality.

Mr. Smith's unique characteristic emerged when he insisted that I was incorrectly spelling and pronouncing my last name. Despite my attempts to clarify and assert the accuracy of my pronunciation, we found ourselves at an impasse. To move forward, we agreed to disagree on this matter, though the encounter left me with a lingering sense of disrespect.

An interesting facet of my academic experience at Dillard University was the prevalent assumption among peers that British English and American English were virtually indistinguishable. This misconception was particularly relevant to me, given my educational background under the British system. The frequent encounters with this misunderstanding provided insight into the general lack of awareness about linguistic differences between the two English variants.

While I navigated the academic challenges with relative ease and found the instructors to be understanding, a different concern weighed heavily on my mind – financial constraints. The constant worry about having enough funds to meet the requirements of my program created a backdrop of uncertainty throughout my university journey.

Within the academic sphere, my classes proceeded without significant issues, and the understanding demeanor of the instructors contributed to a positive learning environment. However, an unfortunate and recurring source of distress emerged in the form of derogatory remarks from some classmates. The phrase "go back to your country" became a disheartening refrain, resurfacing when these classmates faced setbacks or when African students outperformed them on assignments or exams. This unwarranted hostility served as a disruptive force, casting a shadow over the collective experience of international students

The impact of these remarks extended beyond mere discomfort; they posed a considerable distraction, diverting attention from the academic journey and creating an emotional burden. The environment, which should have fostered diversity and collaboration, was tainted by a divisive undercurrent that made it challenging for international students to fully immerse themselves in the university community.

As I reflect on my time at Dillard University, the memories of these experiences linger, influencing not only my academic pursuits but also shaping my understanding of cultural dynamics within educational institutions. The intersections of language, culture, and financial concerns created a complex tapestry of challenges that demanded resilience and perseverance.

Amidst these challenges, the importance of fostering cultural awareness and sensitivity within academic settings became apparent. The need for open dialogues and initiatives to bridge gaps in understanding among students from diverse backgrounds became increasingly evident. It underscored the significance of creating an inclusive environment where students could focus on their academic goals without the burden of unwarranted prejudices.

In retrospect, my journey at Dillard University was a transformative period that encompassed the excitement of academic pursuits, the challenges of cultural misperceptions, and the burden of financial uncertainties. While the academic aspects were managed with determination and the support of understanding instructors, the social and cultural dimensions brought unexpected hurdles. The lasting impact of these experiences emphasizes the ongoing importance of fostering inclusivity, understanding, and support within the diverse tapestry of university communities.

"Not You Two, Just the White Boy"

When I came to the United States my dad gave me my first-year's school fees and made it clear that it was the only school fees that I would be receiving from him since I chose to study outside of Nigeria. So, when I arrived in the United States, I knew that I had to find a job quickly.

After moving off campus, I was able to get a job as a security guard with Bayou State Security. The job involved me being sent to different business locations every few weeks for guard duties. On one occasion, on a very cold rainy day of about 28 degrees, I was posted to AAA Copper Company, off Old Gentilly Road, with two other guards. One was one of my fellow Nigerians, Peter, and the other guard was a white guy. We worked the 7:00 pm to 7:00 am shift that day.

Around 2:00 am it was extremely cold with heavy rain. One of the night managers at AAA Copper Company opened the glass window facing where we were standing under an open overhang and told us to come in from the cold and rain for a cup of coffee.

As Peter and I approached the door he said, "Not you two, just the white boy." We stepped back and the white guard stepped into the office that had a glass view. The white guard was then given a robe to dry off while he joined the manager for coffee and cookies. The two were behind the double glass door and windows in our view pointing and laughing at us standing in the rain and cold.

That night Peter and I wanted to resign, but we stayed because we had to work to pay for school and our other living expenses. We constantly had to remind each other of the reason we came to the United States. It was unfortunate but for us to be successful we had to endure a lot of job discrimination and insults.

The worst part of what happened was that at the end of our shift at 7:00 am, it was still raining, our supervisor, Walden Smith a black man asked the young white guard to get in his truck and gave him a ride home while we had to call for a ride home. There were several incidents of discrimination against us Africans working for Bayou State Security. When we complained and tried to make an official report, we were just told that we can quit and go back to our country.

Since it was difficult to find jobs at that time and we needed the job, we stayed and focused on our goal of earning enough money to pay for school, rent, and take care of ourselves.

While working as a security guard, I also worked as a taxicab driver for Yellow Cab Taxi Company in between my classes, the guard job, and on weekends. Working as a security guard and as a taxicab driver was how I paid for the last three years of my Dillard University college education and living expenses. That was an exceedingly challenging time in my life.

When I was with Bayou State Security, I worked with an interesting man from Milwaukee, Wisconsin named J.J. Ball. We worked as night guards at the Standard Coffee Plant by the Industrial Canal. J.J. spent most of the night shining and waxing his Black Gran Torino. He loved telling me stories about Milwaukee and his time in the service. J.J. had about four of his top teeth missing and loved to chew tobacco; so, it was so funny watching him just talk and spit all at the same time.

Two rascals constantly tried to break into the plant to steal coffee. This always amazed me because they couldn't take a lot on their bikes, so they seemed to just steal for themselves. J.J. had warned the guys on several occasions to stop coming to steal the coffee. They didn't listen and kept coming.

One particular evening when the two guys showed up at the back of the plant, J.J. ran into them while on patrol. He shouted to them that they were to stop coming on the property. He said if they came back, he would shoot them. Their response this evening was to pull out a gun and they shot in J.J.'s direction. J.J. dodged the bullet and shouted that he was calling the police. The guys ran away.

The very next evening, the two guys showed up again. J.J. told them to stop or he was going to shoot them in the ass. One of the guys ignored him and continued accessing the plant. J.J. warned him again. "Stop! or I will shoot you in the ass!" The guy kept coming. When J.J. approached him, he turned to run away but J.J. shot him in the ass, just like he warned him. The guy shouted and screamed, "You shot me in the ass!"

J.J. called the police to report the shooting. The New Orleans Police operator asked J.J. if the man was dead. J.J. told them "no" but he was hopping around. The police told him they would send a unit over. After four hours, the police had not shown up.

The wounded guy just hopped away cursing. J.J. just

laughed and said "Well, New Orleans Police! Never show up when you need them!"

I think about what happened to J.J. occasionally because he was very nice to me. He would give me time to study while working and seemed to care that I would finish school.

And justice for all?

The rain was coming down in relentless sheets; I sat in my Subaru on the side of the road, watching helplessly as my engine sputtered and died. It was a Friday evening, and I was on my way to my shift at the Rodeway Inn in Kenner, just across from the airport. I knew I couldn't afford to be late, but my car had other plans.

I ran across the street to the nearest payphone to call my supervisor, a man of Eastern Indian descent named Raj Singh. I explained my predicament and the dire need for assistance. I expected empathy, understanding, or at the very least, some guidance on what to do next. But what I got in return was a cold and stern voice on the other end of the line.

"If you don't come in, you will be fired," Raj stated matter-of-factly.

I was stunned. It was clear that the rain-soaked roads and my car's failure were beyond my control, yet he showed no sympathy. I tried to reason with him, explaining that I had no means of transportation and was stranded miles away from work. But his response was unforgiving: "It's Friday night, and we're busy. If you're not here, you're done."

With no other choice, I hung up the pay phone and stepped out into the pouring rain. I was drenched within seconds, my clothes sticking to my skin. The eight-mile journey to work seemed like an insurmountable task, but I had to do it. I couldn't afford to lose this job; I had rent and school fees to pay.

Each step I took was a battle against the elements. The rain stung my face, and the wind seemed determined to push me back. But I pressed on, my determination fueling me.

Finally, after what felt like an eternity, I arrived at the Rodeway Inn, completely drenched and exhausted. I could barely recognize myself in the lobby's reflective glass doors. I approached the front desk, hoping for some understanding from Raj. Instead, he glanced at me with a mix of disbelief and disdain.

"You made it," he muttered as if he had expected me to fail. I tried to explain the ordeal I had endured, but he cut me off. "I thought you were lying, trying to get out of work on a busy Friday night. You'll need to change into your uniform quickly."

As I headed to the employee restroom to change, I couldn't help but feel the weight of the discrimination I had faced. I had walked eight miles in a downpour just to keep my job, yet Raj had assumed the worst of me. It was clear that his treatment of me was based on prejudice and bias.

Throughout the shift, Raj continued to treat me poorly, assigning me the most grueling tasks and watching my every move. It was as if he was determined to make my night miserable. But I endured it all because I needed the job.

The next morning my friend Prince Nwaorgu came to pick me up and check on my car. I couldn't help but reflect on the injustice I had faced. It was a stark reminder that discrimination could rear its ugly head in the most unexpected of places and that the fight for fairness and equality was far from over.

My struggles with discrimination and mistreatment were not limited to my experience at the Rodeway Inn. Also, while I was a student at Dillard University in New Orleans, I had another job at Bayou State Security, an opportunity I hoped would help me make ends meet during my academic journey.

At Bayou State Security, I quickly discovered that racial discrimination was deeply ingrained in the company's culture. It was evident from day one that African employees, me included, were treated unfairly. We were often assigned to the worst posts and the most challenging assignments, often in unsafe or unpleasant conditions. This was despite our qualifications and capabilities, which were equal to those of our non-African coworkers.

Perhaps the most blatant form of discrimination was the way they exploited African employees by forcing us to work overtime without providing the extra pay that we deserved. Sometimes I would work 40 hours a week but, when I received my paycheck, they would only pay me for 30 hours. I vividly recall the long and exhausting shifts that were imposed on us, sometimes without any prior notice. We were expected to stay on post long after our scheduled hours had ended, all the while knowing that we would not receive any additional compensation for the extra time and effort we put in.

The discrimination didn't end with unfair working conditions and unpaid overtime. It was disheartening to hear derogatory comments from supervisors and coworkers who believed they could demean us with impunity. When we dared to speak up about the unfair treatment or demand better conditions and fair wages, the response was even more distressing.

Instead of addressing our concerns, we were met with threats, insults, and derogatory remarks. They held this position because many of us did not have the authorized papers to work in the United States but needed to work to support ourselves.

It was not uncommon for those in authority at Bayou State Security to tell us to "go back to Africa" as if that was a legitimate response to our grievances. These hateful comments were not only racist but also deeply hurtful. They got away with this maltreatment and skirting from paying the required employment taxes.

Despite the hardships and the discrimination, I persisted in my efforts to balance work and education. My experiences at Bayou State Security and the Rodeway Inn were stark reminders of the persistent inequalities and injustices that many face. These experiences motivated me to strive for change, not only for myself but for others who were subjected to similar treatment.

Through my determination, I continued my education at Dillard University, and I ultimately found better employment opportunities that treated me with the respect and fairness I deserved. These experiences strengthened my resolve to stand against discrimination and advocate for equal rights and treatment for all, regardless of their race or background.

Destined Hearts: The Day I Met My Future Wife

Despite the uncertainty that I faced coming to the United States and the frustration of trying to explain to Mr. Smith, my then English 101 instructor that I was pronouncing and spelling my last name the right way, attending Dillard University was part of God's divine plan for my life.

During orientation, I was trying to adjust to my new environment. One evening I ventured into the cafeteria to eat some dinner. I sat down at a table by myself and began eating. A group of four girls and one guy came and sat down at the table with me.

To my right sat a young lady. She looked over at me and said, "Hello, my name is Deborah Ford. What is your name?" I told her my name and she immediately noticed I had an accent.

She proceeded to strike up a conversation with me. She asked where I was from and seemed excited that I was from Nigeria. She told me she was from the San Francisco Bay Area, a town named San Mateo. I had no idea where that was at the time.

Deborah then asked me, "How do you say 'Hello' in your language?" I responded by saying, "Wichone." She seemed excited by learning a bit of my language. She kept repeating the word. We then turned our attention back to eating our meal.

After dinner, we went our separate ways. I met Deborah again when she was taking the same biology lab class. I do not recall having any conversation with her during our biology lab class.

At that point, I did not realize that God's plan was in motion shaping the destiny He planned for me. That innocent meeting in the cafeteria was the beginning of our lifelong conversations.

Deborah Joy Ford from San Mateo, California

Deborah and I: Adventures in Love and Laughter

After our dinner encounter, I went to Williams Hall a few days later to visit Deborah. She came down to greet me. I invited her to get something to eat. I drove her to Popeyes to get some chicken. Now my recollection of this event differs from Deborah's. I just remember ordering two chicken meals and pulling forward. But Deborah claims I ordered a two-piece meal for myself and a three-piece for her. She asked why I had ordered her a larger meal, she says I responded, "Big girls like big things." I DO NOT remember!

After getting our meals, we drove back to campus and talked more. Deborah did inform me that she had a boyfriend in Mississippi. We continued talking and decided to remain friends. That was okay with me because loyalty is extremely important to me. I also wanted to focus most of my time on my studies so I could achieve my goal of coming to the United States, graduating with a degree from Dillard University, maybe obtain my master's degree, and return home to Nigeria where I know that I would have a better chance of a successful career. So, I spent a lot of my free time at the library studying before going to work.

Deborah and I continued as friends, and we saw each

other during class. In the fall, we were in the same History, Biology, and Algebra classes. Deborah asked me one day why I only came to Algebra on exam days. I laughed and told her that I had already had all the course content in high school. She was amazed. In the Spring semester, we had PE, History, Biology, Biology Lab, and Calculus classes together. I discovered that, in addition to her beauty, Deborah talked a lot. More than an average person but that was good because she had a lot to say, and I enjoyed listening to her.

Towards the end of January, I noticed a "spike" in the meetings with Deborah in the library. She would "happen" upon me and strike up a conversation. She began talking to me more in class as well. This went on for a couple of months. During one of our conversations, she mentioned that she was available. I guessed she had broken up with her boyfriend though she did not directly say it that way. As for me, I was not available for a relationship because I wanted to concentrate on my studies without distractions. So, I continued to keep it in the friendship zone.

In late April 1983, I had an accident and totaled the first car I had in the U.S. -- a silver Subaru coupe. During one of our library meetups, I told Deborah about the accident. She seemed genuinely concerned. I told her that I was in the market for a new vehicle. She became a new car advisor, suggesting cars I could buy.

I purchased a used 1982 red and gray Dodge Challenger that I liked a lot. When I informed Deborah of my purchase, she seemed to light up. She asked to see it. I showed her and she asked for a ride. I was on the way to work and couldn't at the time, so she suggested another time.

We agreed to go on our first date on Tuesday, May 2nd (this date will be incredibly important later). I did not know where to take her on a first date, but the decision was simple since I had little money and loved Chinese food (which was more affordable). We decided to go to a Chinese restaurant that was not too far from Dillard's campus and near the Gentilly Post Office. After eating at the Chinese restaurant, we stopped at the house of one of my friends, Ngozi Okon. We talked a bit and he asked where we were going. I told him that we were going to the movies. He asked if he could come along. I said sure and he came with us. We went to a movie theater where we saw the movie "Flash Dance."

However, one of my vices then was that I made commentaries during movies. While I enjoyed the movie, I felt that I whispered too much in her ear during the movie and that I may have pushed her away. But it did not push her away, she just sat there and listened or tuned me out. Either way, I enjoyed being at the movie with her.

During college, I wanted to spend Spring Breaks on the beach like the other students, but I had to work and could not do all those things. Deborah didn't seem to mind. She enjoyed the simple things, and I liked her more for that. Most of our other dates were also simple and fun. We went to the parks, picnics on the Lakefront, enjoyed concerts on campus and the dollar movies.

Deborah loved me in this blue velvet jacket!

Deborah and I at the Embassy, Winter 1984

Career Choices

I had a different career path in mind when I arrived at Dillard University. I was an all-rounded student in high school. I excelled in my science, mathematics, and liberal arts classes such as business and accounting. I considered a career in business management, I also wanted to become a physician where I could help take care of people. Medicine has always been my desire.

When I arrived at Dillard University, the school fees for science classes were much higher than the fees for business classes. I knew that I would not be able to finance my education through Dillard and into medical school. In addition, I was ill-advised by my college advisor at that time that only American citizens were allowed into medical schools in the United States. I did not know, nor did I understand the system at that time.

Knowing that my finances were limited, I had no choice but to pursue business administration at Dillard University. This allowed me to have less of a financial burden. Studying business administration became one of the best educational decisions that I made. As it turns out so far, I think I made a good decision. I continued my education earning a master's in business administration with a concentration in Finance from Morgan State University in Baltimore, Maryland, and a Doctorate from Nova Southeastern University in Fort Lauderdale, Florida.

My business career has been good to me and I believe that it was God's plan for me all along. My family and I have been truly blessed by God through this career path.

Graduation... Finally!

Despite the struggles and hardships, I completed my course of study at Dillard University with a bachelor's degree in business administration in May 1986. I am proud to say I finished on time. It was a big relief to me since my goal was to complete my degree program at Dillard.

During the graduation ceremony, I looked back to the time when I met my high school classmate who gave me one of his Dillard University admissions packets saying that he would be going to the "Blue Devils" for his university studies. I had never thought of coming to the United States to further my education or to Dillard University until I met him on that faithful day.

Sitting among fellow new graduates, I also went back in time to when I met Kenneth Iduwonyi who showed me the process of obtaining the required documents which were needed by the United States Embassy to complete the visa application process. He also helped me obtain my first international passport.

My thoughts were everywhere. Mr. Igueze, the accountant at the then New Nigerian Bank in Benin City and one of my father's tenants overheard the conversation I had with my friend, Tony, concerning my Uncle John who was a regional bank manager and refused to help me get the bank draft that I needed to pay for the university application fee. Mr. Igueze helped me by giving me the bank drafts to pay my admission application fee. Then it finally hit me that my time at Dillard University had come to an end.

The graduation ceremony was long as guest speakers and other invited academia gave long boring speeches that most of the graduating class tuned off, including myself. After the long speeches, the names of the graduates were called to come to the stage and receive their diplomas. When my name was called, I was excited to finally receive my diploma but a little sad that none of my family members could attend my graduation since they were all back home in Nigeria.

However, the most important people in my life were there cheering me on. My girlfriend Deborah (now my wife) and Auntie Rosalie Green (now resting in the Lord). I completed my education at Dillard University with no fees owed to the school. What a joy!

My graduation picture, Spring 1986

My graduation day at Dillard University, May 1986.
Deborah and Aunt Rosalie Green attended.

Fair Dillard?

"Fair Dillard" is a line from the alma mater. Well, Dillard was not fair to me! My days at Dillard University were days of struggle and hardship. I was always trying to balance my school and work schedule to achieve my goal of graduating with a bachelor's degree from Dillard. Those times were hard. My class schedule mostly ran from 8:00 am to 4:30 pm. I went to the library after class for a few hours to study and do my assignments before going to my looked forward to going on campus to meet Deborah. She had her way of making things easier. She loved the navy blue and burgundy velvet jackets I used to wear those days. I found it interesting that she was fascinated by apartment to get some rest. Then at 10:00 pm I'd get up and get ready to report for work at 11:00 pm.

During the weekdays, I mostly worked from 11:00 pm to 7:00 am then rushed home to get ready for my 8:00 am class. On the weekends, I worked from 7:00 pm to 7:00 am, however I did get a day off on a rotating weekend. That didn't leave me a lot of time for socializing but at "The Embassy" we made it all work out for us by getting together on weekends and some early evenings when time permitted.

Despite the hardship, I was always dressing up for class. I could not help that since I had been trained and conditioned to dress up for class since my high school days.

She asked me on several occasions why I did not wear casual clothing to class so, I eventually hung up the jackets and wore more casual clothing to class, just for her.

I was not happy with the manner in which Dillard University treated some of the African students during my time at Dillard. We were treated like ATMs. To sum it all up, Dillard University's management was not fair to me and most of the other African students.

Just to give you one example: My father paid for my first year at Dillard by cashier's check. Once all the fees were deducted, there was a $2400 balance. I was called to the Bursar's Office and when I arrived, I was asked to sign the refund check back to the school. I needed the money, and I told the bursar this fact. She was adamant that I needed to sign the check to the school. She flipped the check over and held the check. There was a glass partition with a small opening between us; I tried to sign but couldn't as she gripped the check. I was able to get the check from her and said, "Thank you!" I quickly walk away from the window and down the hall. She was shouting at me to come back with the check or else. I just ignored her and left.

When I went to deposit the check at my bank, Whitney Bank, a few days later and withdrew some cash, the teller told me the funds were on hold and could not be touched. I knew something was up. I demanded my money, they said "no" and they were going to call Dillard. So, I told the lady to close my account immediately and give me all my funds in cash. She had no choice but to honor my request. It is for that reason that to this day, I never banked with Whitney Bank again!

Pastor Charles Green and Word of Faith Church

When I was at Dillard University, there was a group of Christian brothers and sisters I met during my first semester at school. We would get together for prayer meetings at the chapel for about one or two hours once a week. Occasionally we would visit Southern University in Baton Rouge and join another group of Christian brothers and sisters there and fellowship with them during their meeting time.

During our time at Southern University, we connected with a brother who had a fiancée studying at Dillard. They extended an invitation to Pastor Charles Green, the Senior Pastor at Word of Faith Church, to join us in one of our prayer meetings. Pastor Charles Green, after attending, graciously invited us to visit his church. Intrigued, I decided to attend, and I found joy in worshiping there because Christ and the Word of God were central to the preaching. Following numerous visits, I decided to formally become a member of Word of Faith Church in New Orleans.

Throughout my time at Word of Faith, I took on the role of a Bible foundation teacher, dedicating my Sundays to instructing others and actively engaging in the fellowship of the men's group. This commitment persisted for over two decades, underscoring my enduring connection and involvement within the church community.

A Forever Promise: The Day I Proposed

I previously stated many times that I was not going to get married until I was in my thirties. In 1986, Deborah and I had been dating for three years while in college. I planned to attend New York University for my graduate studies. Deborah had one more semester at Loyola University in New Orleans. She had transferred to Loyola from Dillard after her freshman year.

Well, I changed my mind about getting married in my thirties. On May 2, 1986, I proposed to Deborah when we were at my Frenchman's Wharf's apartment complex sitting on the couch watching a movie. May 2nd was an important date, as it was the date of our first "official" date that first spring in college. And she said "Yes." We then decided to get married only after she graduated from Loyola. The proposal was nothing elaborate. It was simple, and simple was good.

Me and the future Mrs. Irabor

The Road to 'I Do': Preparing for the Big Day

It turned out, May 2, 1987, was on a Saturday. So, we chose this date as our wedding date. The preparation for our wedding took an act of God's intervention to make all the plans a success. In every wedding plan, I have now found that there are hidden costs that manifest themselves at a very unrealistic time. I had planned to get married with no full knowledge of what goes into wedding preparation as regards the cost.

First, we came up with a budget for the wedding and realized that we did not have enough money for the basic items such as a wedding dress and other things needed. I decided to get another job working as a car parking attendant in a car garage in the French Quarter. I designated all the money that I earned to help pay for the wedding since my parents lived in Nigeria and were not able to help with any of the expenses. My fiancé's parents did not initially help either.

We purchased rings from Service Merchandise. We were able to put them on layaway and pay them off after four months. Our budget for the wedding gown was four hundred dollars. So, Deborah and I went first to all the bridal shops in New Orleans, Metairie, and Gretna. They were so expensive for our budget! Then we went to Dillard's in the Lake Forest Plaza. They had the perfect dress and veil for Deborah, and it fell just below our budget. We were both incredibly happy.

For our honeymoon, we decided to go to Montego Bay. Jamaicia. We contacted a travel agent, and she helped us choose a package for around $750. We were able to make installment payments, so that was checked off the list.

After paying for some of the wedding items, God Almighty intervened on our behalf and showed us favor in many ways that helped us with the wedding planning for items we needed such as the flowers and decoration items that were donated to us by a fellow church member and from a wedding they attended.

On a more dramatic note, we received $500 that was deposited into our bank account from an unknown person (maybe an angel). We needed money to finish paying for the wedding and our honeymoon. I went to Secor Bank to deposit my paycheck. After I made the deposit, the deposit receipt showed an additional $500 in the account balance. I informed the cashier that there was a mistake in my account balance and I did not have an additional $500 in my account. She then double-checked my account and confirmed that the bank balance was correct. After I left the bank, I asked Deborah if she made the deposit, and her answer was no. I then asked her if she knew anyone who would deposit the money in our account, and she said no.

After a few days, I visited the bank and asked for my account balance again and the money was still in the account. This time I asked to speak with a customer service officer at the bank. I then explained to the customer service officer that there was an extra $500 in my account balance, and it was not my money. She then excused herself from our meeting and went behind the counter to check my account information with what she saw on her desktop computer in front of her.

After several minutes she came back with a copy of the deposit slip and said you made the deposit in person. After looking at the deposit slip, I told her you can tell that was not my handwriting. I knew that was not Deborah's handwriting. I instructed her to debit the amount out of my account, insisting the money was not mine and that the bank had made a mistake. She promised to investigate the source of the deposit before I left the bank.

A week later I returned to the bank to speak with the same customer service officer to see if the issue had been resolved. She continued to insist that the money was mine. I now sensed that she was frustrated with the issue. She probably thought that I was crazy or just trying to frustrate her.

At this time, I requested to speak with the bank branch manager. The customer service officer then proceeded to the manager's office which was enclosed in glass, so I was able to see their interactions. After about five minutes the bank manager came out to meet with me and asked me to come with her to her office. She stated that the $500 deposit was made by someone who walked into the bank and made the deposit, and the money was mine and available for immediate withdrawal. She said she would appreciate it if I just accepted the fact that the money was mine and stopped coming to the bank with the issue. I then asked her to fill out the withdrawal slip for my signature. She did and I withdrew the money and used it for our wedding expenses. The money helped us pay our outstanding wedding bills and contributed to our honeymoon.

Deborah's cousin, Sherry Young was instrumental in making our reception a big hit! She prepared all the delicious food to serve our guests. She came down from Lumberton, MS, and put it all together. Deborah's mom took care of the Pastor's gift. Deborah had been working at Sears Automotive in the Plaza and the manager of Budget Rent-A-Car, Eric, gave us a white Lincoln Continental to use for the entire day. Ronnie Fuller, my new brother-in-law, did the driving. That was an interesting time and God is still doing miracles in our lives today. What a blessing!

From the left: Brenda Husband, the late Rachel Hayes, and Sherry Young. Sherry helped us by cooking a marvelous spread.

Our Perfect Beginning: The Wedding Day Story

When May 2, 1987, finally came, we were married at Word of Faith Church on the I-10 Service Road off Bullard Blvd. in New Orleans. With all the pre-wedding preparations, the wedding day finally arrived, and I was very nervous. As always, I wanted everything to be perfect; from starting on time to the reception. Rev. David Newell, a pastor at our church, Word of Faith Church officiated the ceremony.

With all the groomsmen and bridesmaids on the altar, we all waited for my bride's entrance. I remember that my legs were shaking, and my palms were sweating. I had to keep reminding myself that everything was going to be alright. When Deborah started walking down the aisle with her father, what an entrance it was! She looked so beautiful in her white wedding gown; at that point, nothing mattered anymore. My worries disappeared and everything was perfect.

While our ceremony was at the new church building, the reception was at the old church on Read Blvd. Deborah's Dad handed me one thousand dollars and said, "Congratulations." I was grateful but I was thinking we could have used that money while planning the wedding! However, this allowed us to have savings instead of a negative balance in our bank account.

It was a beautiful ceremony. It was not just a beautiful ceremony; it was a beautiful day!

Our wedding party, May 2, 1987

Montego Bay, Jamaica

After the wedding we honeymooned in Montego Bay, Jamaica. Though we had very little money, we had planned for it by both of us taking second jobs and saving as much as we could. We booked a regular King room in our package.

When we arrived at the hotel in Montego Bay, we checked into a room. The room was dark and dingy. I looked into Deborah's eyes and saw the disappointment. The porter also saw the look on her face. He suggested that we move to the Honeymoon Suite. He said it would only cost an additional fifteen dollars per night. Now knowing we had savings to go home to, I felt it was a great deal.

They went up to show us the new room. It was a 360-degree change! The room was large and had a magnificent view from the huge windows. The balcony had a fantastic view of the ocean. There was a large four-poster bed. We felt like this was a classic bait-and-switch situation, but we jumped at the chance!

However, during the change of room, my toiletry bag was stolen. It is a funny story now as it was then because I did not let the unfortunate events affect our honeymoon. It was our first trip to Jamaica.

We enjoyed the beautiful beaches, waterfalls, wonderful food, and the hospitality of the great people of Jamaica for seven days.

Deborah and I on our way to Montego Bay, Jamaica
for our honeymoon, May 1987

The hotel we stayed at in Montego Bay.

"Catch Up With Your Gang!"

Ernest Green, Sr., "Uncle Green," as I knew him, was an interesting man. We first met when my wife introduced me to him as her boyfriend when we were in college. During that first visit he stared at me and asked where I was from and I told him a little bit about myself; basically, that I was a student at Dillard University from Nigeria in West Africa. Ever since that day he never called me by my name. He always referred to me as "The African."

I liked him as soon as I met him. He was funny and reminded me of one of my uncles back in Nigeria. On occasions when I had free time, I would stop by his house to check up on him and we would sit and have conversations about how my education was coming along and New Orleans or African politics.

On the surface, Uncle Green looked rough and had his way of doing things but deep inside he was a kind man I saw through the roughness he projected, and I knew he loved talking to me and having me around.

There once was a time that I was busy and unable to visit with him for over four weeks, when I finally visited with him, he was so glad to see me. With a big smile, he said, "The African is here! Where have you been? I thought you had forgotten about me!" He was a big teddy bear and that was how I saw him.

Uncle Green's love could be seen through his actions. He loved my wife and children as well as "The African." He even had the opportunity to meet my mother when she visited the United States in 1994. We started calling him "Papa LoLo" because he would always tell everyone to "Catch up with your gang!" He would always say what was on his mind. When I remember Uncle Green, he was a good and interesting man. Continue to rest in the Lord, Uncle Green.

Life's Next Chapter: The Moment I Learned I'd Be a Dad

Deborah and I had been married a little over a year when I found out that I was going to be a father. I was very happy. I came to the United States not knowing anyone; I had to struggle and find ways to better myself and now I was going to be a father. I felt that I had made significant progress in life. I was very excited about the news and felt complete. However, the process of pregnancy was tough, especially for my wife as well.

On one occasion, around 9 pm, my wife was craving a banana split ice cream sundae, and she asked if I would go get one for her from Baskin Robbins. I drove to the nearest Baskin Robbins, and they were closed. I continued my search by driving around looking for an open location and finally found a store that was closed but an employee was visible to me from the glass door and windows. I knocked to get the attention of the employee who was now irritated that I would not go away but continued knocking. He finally came to the door, and I explained to him that my wife was pregnant with our first child and wanted a banana split. He looked at me as I continued to plead with him to sell me a banana split ice cream sundae. He finally agreed to sell it to me for $60.

I was excited to be able to get her the banana split from the Carrollton store. When I got home, she was fast asleep, so I placed it in the freezer. The next morning, I told her that I got her the banana split that she asked for but when I got home, she had fallen asleep. She went to the freezer, picked it up continued to look at it, and said, "I cannot stand the smell," and threw it in the trash can. Pregnancy was a process that made our lives interesting.

I always wanted to do well but the news of having a child made me want to do better by making sure that I could make the life of my wife, child, and or children better. I never wanted them to have to endure what I went through in my early years when I first came to the United States. The pain and suffering of not knowing where your next meal was coming from or if you would be able to pay your rent and keep the roof over your head while going to school was something I never wanted my children to experience.

My perspective in life changed when my wife got pregnant with our first child. It made me view the world in a different way knowing that children are a gift from God that must be cared for. To this day, I still feel the same way.

My first son, Mark Irumudomon Irabor, Jr.
At Faith Church Spring of 1989.

My second son, Daniel Abumere Irabor.
At Biloxi Beach Spring 1995

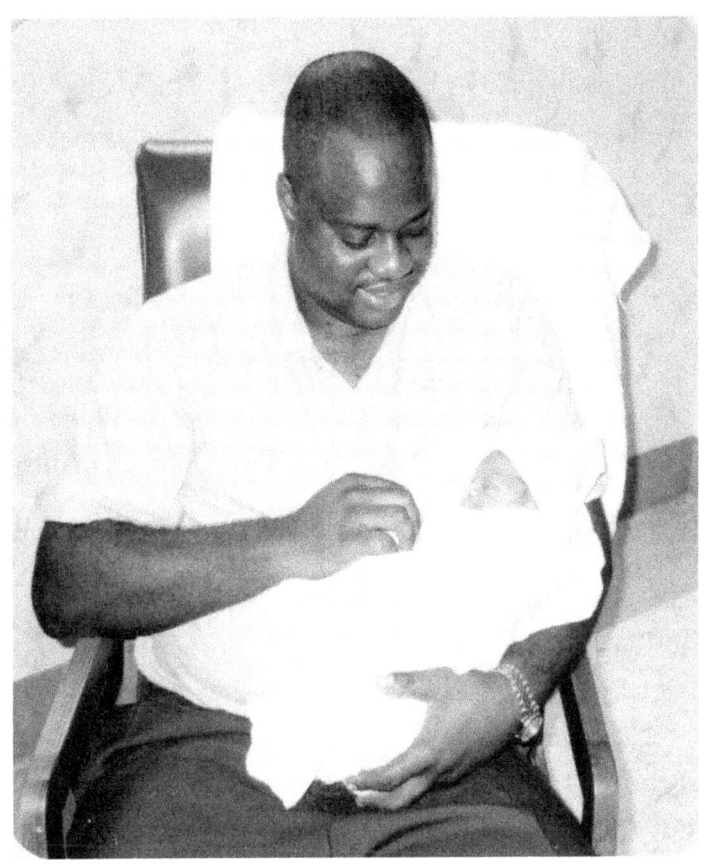

My third son, Michael Eromosele Irabor.
At Lakeland Hospital June 1998.

My Silo, Inc. Days

After I got married, I began working for a company called Silo, Inc., which was located on the Westbank Expressway in Harvey, Louisiana (outside the New Orleans Metro area). It was a place where dreams were born, ambitions were nurtured, and friendships were forged. I was about to embark on a journey that would forever change my life as I assumed a managerial position, overseeing the Computer Department at Silo, Inc. My manager was Doug Mahaffey, who was racist and, in many instances, used the n-word like it was not a big deal. However, the other team members I was fortunate to work with were a diverse and talented group of individuals.

Gina Brown was the heart of the department, a brilliant mind with an infectious smile that could light up even the dreariest of days. Clayton Strickland was our quiet colleague; he was a great listener. Prince Nwaorgu brought a unique perspective to the team with his international background and exceptional problem-solving skills. Wilbert Vincent was a seasoned professional, providing invaluable insights and guidance to the rest of us. And then there was Lee Spalding, the unhappiest and grumpiest person I had ever met.

Lee had worked for Sears Roebuck and Company for decades. Sears forced his retirement and gave him a gold wristwatch. He wore that watch every day and complained about it and Sear's unfairness. It seemed like every day was just another day of misery for him. He was the perpetual cloud that loomed over our otherwise sunny department. Despite his gloomy disposition, we were determined to make the best of our time together.

To balance out the quirks of our team, we had Reuben Williams. He was the source of daily entertainment. Reuben's crazy antics were legendary, from his impromptu breakdancing performances in the breakroom to his absurd yet amusing pranks. Reuben was a living, breathing reminder that work could be fun, even when you had Lee Spalding as a colleague.

As we faced challenging projects, my team's diversity became our greatest asset. Gina's creativity, Clayton's patience, Prince's analytical thinking, and Wilbert's experience formed a formidable combination. Even Lee Spalding, despite his gruff exterior, had an unmatched attention to detail and dedication to his work. Reuben's antics provided moments of levity that broke the tension during long workdays.

Over time, I noticed a change in Lee. He began to smile occasionally, offer a kind word, and even share a joke or two. The transformation was slow, but it was a testament to the positive and supportive environment we had created. It was a remarkable moment when I realized that we had managed to chip away at the wall of misery that had surrounded Lee for so long. He even shared a story that he was a college roommate to former United States Representative from Louisiana, Bob Livingston. While Livingston was studying hard, Lee was getting drunk and enjoying the ladies. So, he had to drop out. Every time the Congressman appeared on the television;

Lee would shake his head commenting that it could have been him.

Reuben continued to be the life of our department, and his antics became a source of inspiration. His fearless approach to life encouraged us to embrace spontaneity and laughter in our everyday work. Our team had truly become a close-knit family, supporting each other through thick and thin.

My time as the Computer Department Manager at Silo, Inc. on the Westbank Expressway was an unforgettable chapter in my career. I had the privilege of leading an incredible team and witnessing the transformative power of a positive work environment. Lee Spalding's gradual shift towards contentment served as a powerful reminder that with patience and determination, even the unhappiest souls can find happiness within a team

As for Reuben, he remained the crazy and lovable character who reminded us all that work could be a place of joy and camaraderie. Silo, Inc. was indeed a great place to work, not just for the opportunities it provided but for the incredible people who made every day an adventure.

Over time, members of the team moved on to different career paths. I went to Baltimore, Maryland to pursue my MBA. Ginger Brown moved to Southern California. Prince Nwaorgu eventually obtained his Doctor of Pharmacy degree and moved to Dallas. We are still friends today.

Clayton Strickland got married and took a managerial position in North Carolina. Wilbert Vincent remained at Silo and stayed in the same industry. He passed shortly after Hurricane Katrina. Lee Spalding eventually retired again and passed a short time later. But the biggest surprise to us all was Reuben Williams became an FBI Agent!

My Road to Graduate School

My longstanding aspiration was to attain an advanced degree following the completion of my bachelor's program. During my final year at Dillard, I aspired to enroll in New York University Graduate School. Nevertheless, I deferred my attendance for various reasons, with financial constraints, notably a lack of funds, being a key factor that hindered my pursuit of a master's program at that time.

However, after graduating from college and working for several years, I decided to pursue my dream of obtaining a master's degree. I then spoke to one of my old friends, Fidelis, who had lived in New Orleans and moved to Baltimore after obtaining his bachelor's degree. He told me he was in the Master of Business Administration degree program at Morgan State University. He encouraged me to apply and offered to allow me to stay with him in his apartment until I could get my place. That was such a blessing, and we are friends to this day.

I applied to Morgan State University as he suggested, and I was offered an interview to meet with the graduate admission committee for the required interview before a final decision was made. Before leaving for Baltimore, I did not feel well. I called and told Fidelis my situation and he encouraged me to still come and attend the interview because if I did not attend the interview, the probability of rescheduling the interview was slim.

My wife, Deborah, was worried since she knew I was sick and that the eighteen-hour drive to Baltimore from New Orleans would be difficult. I insisted that I would be fine because I did not want to lose the only opportunity, I had to go to graduate school. The next day she packed me snacks and drinks for the trip and off I went to a slow start of the drive from New Orleans to Baltimore. It was one of the longest drives of my life. I was not 100% health-wise and worried about what the admission committee would determine regarding my admission.

Upon my arrival in Baltimore, I felt so ill, I had to go to the emergency room at the local hospital. After the examination and tests, I was told I had chicken pox. I was concerned for Fidelis' health chickenpox as I did not want to get sick because of me. When I called him, he told me that he already had chickenpox and was immune and encouraged me to come on.

After the hospital visit, I stayed with Fidelis as planned and went to Morgan State University the next day for the interview. The interview was about one hour long. During the interview, there were three admissions committee members. I stayed my distance and apologized to the committee members for being sick. I expressed my desire to attend Morgan State University Graduate School of Business and stated that was the reason I drove from New Orleans, Louisiana to attend the interview even when I was ill.

The admission committee members were very impressed with my determination to drive to Baltimore in such a condition to attend the interview. Dr. Gatewood, Professor of Strategic Management, and Dr. Subramaniam,

Chair of the Graduate School of Business both voiced how they were impressed with me and congratulated and welcomed me to Morgan State University Graduate School of Business.

I was also offered the Frank C. Decosta Scholarship. Though not enough to pay for my entire program, it helped with my costs of attending Morgan State and I was grateful.

Good Times at Morgan State University

When I arrived and started my graduate program at Morgan State University, I stayed with my friend Fidelis for a few weeks before I was able to get a studio apartment with a recommendation from him in the same apartment building on Lodestone Way, that he used to live in when he arrived in Baltimore few years earlier. Fidelis was a great host, and I appreciated his assistance.

Living in Baltimore was quite an experience from living in New Orleans. The culture of the people in the eastern part of the country was different and fast-paced. It was a melting pot compared to New Orleans at that time. The cold weather took some getting used to.

One of the memories I had about going to graduate school in Baltimore was in Dr. Gatewood's Strategic Management class.

The night before a class test, it started snowing. Dr. Gatewood had told the class that everyone must be present to take the test and no makeup test would be given. He further stated that an absence from the test will trigger an automatic failure from the class. Now, it was previously announced that a snowstorm was coming but nothing prepared me for what I saw in the morning.

The night before I experienced my first snowstorm it

was extremely cold, and it started snowing. When I looked out of the window, a golf-sized hail was falling, and I was amazed at the size of the hail. Now, in the morning when I walked outside my apartment, everywhere was covered in snow which made driving dangerous if not impossible. It was also difficult to shovel the pile of snow on the parked cars in the parking lot. But the scene was so beautiful, and I had a test to take in Dr. Gatewood's class.

I decided to walk to school which was about three miles from my apartment building. I figured that Dr. Gatewood himself would not be coming to give the test, but I was wrong. When I got to class, he was sitting on his chair waiting to start the test. There were about twenty students in his class and only nine showed up for the test. At exactly 10:00 am (test time), Dr. Gatewood started teaching instead of giving us a test. He stated that in managing a business there are going to be external forces that test your resolve and bad weather was one of them. He continued that decision and business governance must continue even in the worst situation. He then said the test was now over and the nine of us that came to class passed his class and he failed the other eleven students that did not show up. They had to wait another year to take his class which was a requirement in completing the graduate program.

However, the best memories that I have from going to school in Baltimore were when my wife came with my son, Mark, Jr. to visit. He was about one and a half years old, and it snowed the day before they arrived. They were fascinated by the snow. We went outside by the field close to my apartment and we were running around and playing in the snow. Mark. Jr. may not remember that now because he was so young. We had a great time and he loved it.

Mark Jr. and I on Morgan's Alumni Memorial Gate 1990.

My family visited me in Baltimore, in 1990.

My Love for Numbers

During my graduate school years, I had the opportunity to work in the operations department at Signet Bank in Baltimore, Maryland. As a financial analyst, my days were filled with spreadsheets, data analysis, and the thrill of crunching numbers. It was a role that not only aligned perfectly with my studies but also ignited my passion for finance.

The atmosphere in the operations department was bustling and collaborative, with a team of dedicated professionals who shared my enthusiasm for financial analysis. I found myself immersed in projects that challenged my skills and expanded my knowledge. The days often stretched late into the evening as I delved into intricate financial reports, striving to extract meaningful insights.

As time passed, the Senior VP took notice of my dedication and skill. She recognized my potential and encouraged me to consider a long-term career at Signet Bank. The prospect was enticing, but it meant remaining in Baltimore, far from my family in New Orleans.

Graduation day arrived, and as much as I had grown to love my job and the city of Baltimore, I knew that my heart belonged to my family in New Orleans. They had supported me throughout my academic journey, and it was time for me to return the favor.

Torn between professional opportunities and the love I felt for my family, I made the difficult decision to head back to New Orleans. It was a bittersweet departure from Signet Bank, a place where I had learned so much and grown both personally and professionally. The Senior VP expressed her disappointment but understood my choice and stated that there would always be a place for me at Signet Bank.

Though I returned to my family in New Orleans, the experiences and knowledge I gained at Signet Bank would forever shape my career and my passion for numbers. The memories of those days in the operations department will always remain a cherished chapter in my journey, reminding me of the love I have for finance and the importance of family.

I Ain't Moving!

In the winter of 1990, after completing my MBA degree program, I was eagerly seeking post-graduate employment. My heart raced with anticipation as I scanned through job listings and attended interviews, all in the hope of finding the perfect opportunity. Then, one fateful day, I received a phone call that would change the course of my life.

The voice on the other end of the line offered me a position as a financial analyst at American Can, a well-established company based in Buffalo, New York. The job promised new challenges and growth opportunities, and I accepted without hesitation. My excitement knew no bounds; I was ready for this next chapter in my career.

As the weeks passed, American Can prepared to move me, my wife, Deborah, and our son, Mark, Jr. from our cozy apartment in New Orleans to Buffalo. They generously helped in finding housing and ensured that the transition would be as smooth as possible. We began the process of packing up our lives in the warm, vibrant city of New Orleans.

One evening, as we were diligently wrapping up our glassware and packing our belongings, the national news channel blared on the television. The headline sent shockwaves through our world: "Historic Blizzard Expected to Hit Buffalo, New York." The anticipation of moving to a colder climate had always been daunting, but this news was on a whole new level.

Deborah looked over at me with a mix of disbelief and determination, and she put down the glass cup she was holding. She proclaimed, "I ain't moving to Buffalo!"

The image of a colossal blizzard burying Buffalo in the snow had sparked fear in her heart, and she was ready to dig in her heels. I could see her hesitation, and deep down, I couldn't deny that I shared some of her concerns. We had always been accustomed to the warmth and vibrancy of New Orleans, and the idea of battling through one of the worst blizzards in history was daunting, to say the least.

We spent hours debating our options. On the one hand, there was this incredible job opportunity that could potentially set us on a path to financial success and professional growth. On the other hand, there was the comforting familiarity of our lives in New Orleans, free from the perils of a record-breaking blizzard.

As the days passed and the blizzard drew nearer, we weighed the pros and cons. The excitement of a new career and the prospect of building a life together in Buffalo battled with the allure of staying in the city we loved. Our hearts and minds were in constant turmoil. Ultimately, we decided to stay in New Orleans for the time being.

A Place to Call Our Own: Our Journey to Homeownership

After living in two apartment complexes over the years, we decided to buy our own home which would provide us with extra living space in a good neighborhood. We drove around several neighborhoods with no success trying to find a house that we liked and could afford.

On Thanksgiving Day in 1993, we were driving around and came across a house at 7105 W. Tamaron Blvd. in a subdivision next to our church, Faith Church, that was for sale. The owners saw us sitting in our car outside their home and looking at their house. They invited us to come in and look inside. We did and loved the house.

When we arrived back home, we discussed the pros and cons of the house and decided to move forward and made an offer to purchase the house. Our offer was accepted by the owners, so we subsequently obtained the financing we needed to buy the house from Liberty Bank in New Orleans. That was how we bought our first home.

Our first home.

The boys and I enjoyed our home, December 1998.

Calling My Own Shots

As far as I can remember I had always wanted to go into business for myself in whatever career path that I landed upon. Growing up, I helped my mother in her distributor business for the Coca-Cola company, beer company, and cement company by driving her pickup truck and making deliveries to her customers. In addition, when she opened a popcorn factory, I helped deliver popcorn to her customers near and far from our hometown.

I also helped my dad when he was building our first home on the construction site clearing the field, learning how to mold bricks, and helping the brick layers move and stack bricks on the site. I hated going to the construction site because we had to wake up early and the job was labor intensive. Little did I know that those experiences were preparing me for the future.

After college, while working in my regular job, I started thinking about different businesses that I would like to go into. I wrote business plans for a computer sales business in which products would be sold internationally, a computer consulting business, a retail shoe store, a tax preparation, and business consulting business. I followed the business plans making inquiries on product lines, supplies, and marketing strategies.

Deciding which business to go into was a little

difficult so I decided to try a couple of them to determine the more lucrative one that I could make a living doing since I intended to eventually work for myself.

From Dream to Reality: Launching My Own Business

The first business that I started was a computer business named Martex International in 1994. Nigeria was behind in the computer industry, so I decided to start Martex International to help fill the void that existed in the computer industries. I purchased about twenty-five Packard Bell computers and shipped them to Nigeria. I then traveled to Lagos, Nigeria since this was my first shipment to meet and develop a customer base for future shipments.

However, upon my arrival, the process of setting up meetings with customers was incredibly challenging after my telephone conversation with them. Their idea was to get the computers from me and pay later after they sold them, which was not the original agreement before the computers were shipped.

One morning while I was in Lagos working on my marketing strategy, my dad who was in Port Harcourt at that time called me and said that his friend who was a senior engineering manager at Shell oil company had decided to purchase all the computers. With the news of the purchase, he sent his driver to pick me up with all the computers in Lagos. A day after we arrived in Port Harcourt, I asked him when we were going to meet with his friend. The story changed to his friend did not have the budget to buy the computers at the time. That was very disappointing because I felt deceived by him when I later found out that his friend never made such a commitment.

He eventually had another friend to look at the computers and they tested all the units to make sure they worked and decided to buy them. I insisted that payment must be made before delivery. But my father insisted that he trusted his friend and I left the computers with my dad in Port Harcourt and went to Benin. After being in Benin for a few days, my dad called that his friend picked up the computers and would be making payment later in the day despite my instructions that payment was to be made before any of the computers were to be distributed.

Payment for the computers was never made as promised and the story behind the payment continues to change. My dad claimed to have been given a payment check but the check was bad. To this day I have never been paid for the computers. It was a complete loss and a disaster. This was an experience that taught me never to deliver products or services without the customer first making a verifiable payment.

I did not pursue the retail shoe business once I found out that the supply chain from China was very unreliable and that will create a lot of problems for me and my future customers. However, I started a tax preparation and consulting business named Global One Educational Consulting. It went well and I had dependable clients and did a lot of work for small business owners, startups, childcare business consulting, business training workshops, business preparation, and tax preparation. While doing all this I was still working full-time in my regular day job.

The "Happy Kids" Story

I began contemplating the creation of a business with enduring viability. One day, during a discussion with my wife about embarking on a new entrepreneurial journey, she expressed her desire to establish a school. This idea sparked intense contemplation, and in the months that followed our conversation, my wife had to travel to California due to her grandmother's serious illness.

During her absence, my mind continued to churn with business ideas. Strangely, I started noticing pregnant women everywhere. It dawned on me – a daycare center. This realization struck me profoundly. Women will consistently welcome new additions to their families, and those engaged in full-time work will inevitably seek a secure environment for the care and education of their infants.

Immediately, I started writing a business plan for a childcare business. I completed the plans in a few days and looked at the numbers (the projected financials) and it made sense to me.

While my wife was still in California, I started driving around the city looking for a viable location for the business. I finally found a house for sale on the corner of Morrison Road and Marywood Court in a residential area that could be used for a childcare business. I asked the owners if the house was still for sale and they said, "Yes."

I asked for a tour of the house if possible and they granted my request. While they were giving me a tour of the house, I saw all the possibilities for the house to be used as a childcare center, so I made an offer to buy the house with plans to remodel it.

When my wife arrived home from her California trip, I picked her up from the airport and drove straight to the house. She asked what was going on and I told her that I had found a house that we could use for school. She took a good look at me and asked, "What school?"

And I replied to her, "A childcare center. You wanted a school, didn't you?"

She answered, "Not this one. I meant a regular school with big kids, not a childcare center."

My response was that everywhere I looked I saw pregnant women and children and these women will need a place that is safe to care for and educate their babies. I further explained to her that with my business experience and her educational background as a teacher (she was a teacher at St. Mary of the Angels Academy at that time) we could make it work and provide a safe place for children. I felt our team would be unbeatable. After listening to me she said it was not what she had in mind. She wanted a school for older kids.

I was not going to proceed if we both did not agree on my idea, but I had already signed an agreement to purchase the property. I figured I had more convincing to do since my initial attempt failed.

Upon our arrival home, we talked about her trip to California and said nothing else on my idea of starting a childcare center. We eventually went to bed.

Around 2:00 am my wife woke me up and said, "I hope you know what you are doing!" She then agreed to move forward with my idea.

Now that she was on board with starting a childcare business, we had to come up with a name for the business. We played around with several names to call the business and my wife came up with the name "Happy Kids Preschool." It was now time to think about all that was required by governmental agencies to make our dream become a reality.

A few days later, I went to the Department of Social Services Licensing and Regulation's Office in Baton Rouge, Louisiana to find out what we needed to do to open a childcare center. I was given the state regulations and guidelines governing childcare centers. Then I proceeded to the Louisiana Department of Health, the Department of Education, and the Fire Marshal's Office and obtained the state regulations guidelines concerning childcare centers. I spent about two months reading the state regulations that govern childcare businesses.

In the meantime, I was also working on getting a contractor and an architect to help us meet the required regulations. However, our funds were almost depleted since we spent most of our savings getting the building and all other necessary startup costs. With our limited resources, it appeared our dream may not be achieved as planned.

While still looking for a contractor, I contacted one of my homeboys who was a contractor to help us with the renovation, but he declined stating that he only worked on million-dollar deals.

I continued my search for a contractor and an architect. I found the name of an architect in the Yellow Pages, Lewis Clements. I called him and explained my situation to him, and he agreed to meet with me. We met a few days after my call, and we discussed the remodeling of the house to accommodate its use as a childcare center and my lack of funds to pay for his services. He was surprised when I told him that I did not have the money to pay him for his services but promised to pay him as soon as I could. Mr. Clements looked at me and laughed and said that I was very funny in that he had never met anyone like me before coming to request his architectural services and said that I did not have any money to pay for the services that I was requesting.

He explained that he was retired but willing to come out of retirement to help me with the architectural drawings to design the floor plan and obtain local operational permits because he felt that it would be interesting to work with me on the project. He agreed and visited our building a few days after our meeting, then we started work on the building renovation plans. He completed the plans as promised and I kept my promise and paid him as soon as I had the money for his fees. I must say he was a pleasant man to work with on the project.

After Mr. Clements completed the building renovation plans, our search for a contractor came to a halt since we did not have the money to get a contractor. As a result, we started doing the renovation work ourselves. We also had help from one of my wife's classmates (Mike) who was a carpenter when she was taking classes for her master's degree program. Mike completed all the carpentry work while I worked on installing drywall and concrete needed for the handicap ramps and other required items that will enable us to open.

Upon completing the renovation, I proceeded to file and obtain the occupational permits and childcare licensing needed to start the childcare operation. The process was more stressful and difficult than I expected but, in the end, we made it work. That was how we started Happy Kids Preschool in June 1996.

After we received the permit from the City of New Orleans and the childcare license from the Louisiana Department of Social Services Licensing and Regulations, we opened our first childcare center.

Our first Happy Kids on Morrison Road, New Orleans, Louisiana which we opened in June 1996.

The first few months were difficult. During the first 30 days, we struggled to have students at the center; we had no students in the first eight weeks of operation. That was challenging since we had spent all our reserve funds to open the center. Even some of our friends who had children opted to take them to other centers instead of supporting us in our new business. That was a surprise to us, especially since we had been friends for a long period and we watched each other's children when needed. It was a lesson in business that I learned to this day; never depend on your friends to support your business endeavors at the infancy stage or beyond.

With cash depleted and now down to $1 between my wife and I, we kept the faith that God will send us some students in the coming weeks. We spent the weekend walking shopping centers parking lots and surrounding businesses placing flyers of our new business on car windows with the hope of generating business.

On the following Monday morning, we had a parent come into the center and register her child into our preschool program. That was our first student nine weeks after we opened. Our tuition was $55 per week and $40 for registration. She paid the tuition for the month and the registration fee for a total of $260. That was the first money we received for our services and with that we were able to buy needed supplies and food for the center. Those were difficult days and I perceived in my spirit that more difficult days were ahead however, we believed that God was going to give us more ideas on how to increase our student registration. I continued to walk the neighborhoods, businesses, and parking lots distributing our business flyers daily.

A few weeks after our new and only student Chad was registered into our program, we had two more registrations and a week later about three additional students. Now with six students, I expanded the areas where I was passing out the flyers and still return to the original shopping center parking lots with my flyer distribution even in the rain.

When we originally applied for a permit to operate, we were told that we could not have a sign on our business property because it was in a residential area. However, there were other businesses further down from our building on the same side of Morrison Road with business signs. I prayed about the sign situation and felt that I should apply for a sign permit. I went to the city permit office to apply for a business sign.

Upon arriving at the city hall for the permit application, I was told that I needed an architectural drawing of the sign. I went back to Mr. Lewis Clements, the architect who had helped us with the renovation plan, and once again without hesitation he helped us prepare the sign drawing and followed up with questions from the permit department.

Mr. Lewis Clements was an architect, a true professional, a gentleman, and a man of compassion and integrity and I believe that God had him in our path to be a blessing to us, helping us through the process.

I submitted the completed sign drawing to the sign permit office and met with one of the senior engineers (Anthony E.) who was in charge of approving the permit, he was also from Nigeria. Anthony frustrated my efforts in obtaining a sign permit by finding everything wrong with the architectural sign plan and tried everything in his power to make sure that I did not get the permit, but God gave us a way to hinder his plans. After several attempts to get the sign permit approved, Anthony asked me to change the drawn sign plan and return for resubmission for another plan review the next day at 3:00 pm. However, God placed in my heart to go to the permit office during lunchtime at noon the next day instead of 3:00 pm with the same plan that Anthony refused to accept for approval.

The next day I went to the plan permit office during lunch time with the same plan and requested to speak with anyone for plan review. I was immediately brought to the office where the engineering manager in charge of plan review was, and he reviewed my plan and approved it for the issuance of the sign permit.

As I departed, I encountered Anthony who was just returning from lunch. He appeared surprised to find me exiting his department and inquired about my early arrival. I explained that I had obtained the necessary approval from the engineering manager for the sign permit, to which he reacted with surprise. After thanking him for his assistance, I continued with my tasks.

I proceeded to the sign company and paid for a sign to be made for Happy Kids. After the sign was completed, I picked it up and installed it myself in the front yard of our building.

A few days after the sign installation, our telephone started ringing and prospective parents started calling and visiting the center which led to more student enrollment. Deborah and I could no longer handle the day-to-day operations by ourselves, so we hired our first employee Adrianne LaRoche. Adrianne was calm and loved working with the infants. I worked as the cook, computer teacher, and maintenance person, Deborah worked with the other children in the classroom as a teacher.

Now, with over thirty students enrolled and more prospects in the works, we hired more employees. The installation of the sign immediately created a problem with our next-door neighbor Charlie. He started calling the permit office stating we had an illegal sign installed in front of our building. Charlie was told that we did have an approved sign permit for the sign issued by the City of New Orleans.

Charlie became a constant nuisance with his ringing of the doorbell to complain about the noise level coming from the center, even when the children were taking a nap. On one occasion, a photography sales lady visiting our center accidentally parked her car in his driveway and Charlie proceeded to park his car behind the lady's car and refused to move his car for hours. Charlie was then joined by another neighbor, Jimmy, who lived behind the center. They both gave us a lot of problems.

It was frustrating because across from our center a

man used his home garage as a mechanic shop, which was unlicensed and none of the neighbors complained. Charlie and Jimmy approached parents of children at our center and made a lot of false statements about our center. I was frustrated and began to question if we were in the right place and doing the right thing. Choosing not to give up, we continued in prayers and asked the Lord for direction and affirmation.

One morning while in my office, the doorbell rang at the front door facing Morrison Rd. (we rarely used this entrance). As I opened the door an old white lady in a white gown was standing in front of me and I greeted her and asked her to come in. She responded that she would not be long as she was sent to give me a message. She then said, "The Lord wanted you to know that you are doing the right thing and that everything was going to be alright." I asked her to wait so I could get my wife. I rushed to get Deborah and asked her to come quickly to hear what this old lady was saying. As we returned to the door she was gone.

We looked everywhere and I walked down the street but could not find her. At that moment I realized that God had sent an angel in the form of an old lady to give us the assurance we needed.

Despite the neighbor's efforts to make things difficult for us, the Lord continued to bless our efforts, and in a short period, we reached our licensed capacity of forty-three students. A little over a year after we opened, we had a waiting list of parents who wanted to place their children in our center, but we were at full capacity. In addition, several of our current parents were pregnant and we had to place them at the top of the waiting list.

Some of the expecting parents started complaining

that they expected their newborns to be accepted into our school when they turned two months old (which was the age we started accepting children). While contemplating how to handle our space issue having enough space, every time I went out, I started seeing a lot of pregnant women again. I felt that God was trying to tell me something by opening my eyes to see all the pregnant women. I then felt the need to open another center, a much bigger center with enough capacity to handle our waiting list and current pregnant families.

I developed a business plan that built on what we were doing and where we would like to be in the future about the services we offered. We felt the plan must benefit our current parents, future parents and the community at large.

I also wanted a building that would reflect God's blessings in our lives. Again, I started driving around the neighborhood looking for land for sale in areas that were a walking distance to bus stops with a good traffic flow and were close to apartment complexes. After a few months, I found land on Read Boulevard close to Morrison Road and it felt like a perfect area for our second location and not too far from our first location.

Most people were staying away from developing this part of Read Boulevard, but I felt the peace of God to go ahead and purchase the land. I contacted the owners and made an offer below the asking price of the land and waiting for a higher counteroffer, but the owners accepted our initial offer on the condition that we deposit $10,000 and complete the purchase no later than three weeks or we lose the deposit and sale. I requested more time to complete the land deal, but the seller was in a hurry to close the deal and refused to grant us more time.

That was a very short time trying to get financing for the land, but I accepted the conditions. We were able to complete the land purchase in the timeframe the sellers wanted.

Exactly seven days after signing the closing documents for the land, Walgreens made a big announcement that they would be building a new pharmacy just a block away from the land. The land values doubled after Walgreen's announcement and the people that we bought the land from called me and offered to buy the land back from us for what we paid for it plus $50,000 in profit. We refused. God had worked the land deal in our favor.

This is the land we purchased on Read Blvd. near Morrison Road. The top photo was the rear view of the land. The bottom photo is the view facing Read Blvd.

Now that we owned land for the second Happy Kids location, we had to build the building which had a projected construction cost of $500,000 and a designed capacity that would at least double our first location of 43-children capacity. That was in 1997.

I called Mr. Lewis Clements again because I needed a full construction plan drawn for our new building. He agreed to meet with me, and I told him about our plans to build a new facility, my building design idea, and that at least now I can afford to pay him. He laughed and said, "Mark, I am retired!" I pleaded with him to come out of retirement just one more time to help us make our dream of constructing our new building come true. He did and we worked on my vision of what the building layout should look like.

While Mr. Clements was working on the building plans, I started talking to a builder whom I met in the men's prayer meeting in church named Donald Carriere. I explained our project and he agreed to take the job as the contractor to build the building. I also told him that I was interested in shadowing him in the construction process so I could learn about building construction.

At first, he hesitated and said that I would drive him crazy on the job site but in the end, he agreed. I told him as soon as I got an approved plan and a loan for the building project, I would let him know so he can have our project on his schedule.

It took about two months for Mr. Clements and me to finish the new architectural plans and we moved forward with the submission to the City of New Orleans Permit Office and subsequently getting the approval from the building permit office.

Getting a construction loan for the project was more challenging than I expected. It seemed almost impossible. I went from one bank to another presenting our business plan in support of a construction loan with no success. I ended up going to twenty-three banks and they all turned us down for a construction loan with no specific reason given to me. One of the banks that turned us down was a minority-owned bank, Liberty Bank. The Senior Vice President of the bank told me, "It's not like if you build it, they will come!" He went on to advise me to rent a building that would give me the same capacity stating that the rent would only be about $5,500 per month. As a student of finance and having once worked in the bank, my response to him was if the bank loaned us the money our monthly payment would only be $4,500 per month with the prevailing interest rate. He looked at me and said, "Sorry, we cannot do it."

I met with another Sr. VP of commercial lending at a bank on Causeway Blvd. in Metairie who showed what I thought was a great interest in our loan presentation by promising to take a deeper look at our business plan. He then asked me to come back for a 9:00 am meeting the following day. I arrived at the bank early the next day excited that we might finally get our loan request approved. I waited in the waiting lobby from 8:45 am until 1:00 pm when his secretary finally told me that I would not be meeting with the VP. He left on vacation that Friday morning. I told the secretary I was confused as to why he would ask me to meet with him if he knew that he was not going to be in the office. She then said she was sorry that he was not going to approve the loan because he threw the business plan in the trash without looking at it as soon as I left his office the day before. She again apologized for not telling me earlier and was sorry that I had to wait for nothing.

Several other bankers would not even meet with me and one suggested that I can go to a minority bank and ask for a business loan since I was a minority. The twenty-third bank that I went to was First Bank in downtown New Orleans on Poydras Street. After reviewing our business plan the loan officer asked me to come back in a few days for him to meet with the loan committee before he could give me an answer. I went back a week later and during our meeting, he told me that the committee was very impressed with the business plan, but they would not move forward with loan approval. I was frustrated so I asked him what was wrong with my business plan and pleaded with him to tell me the truth so I could make changes and not make the same mistake again.

I asked for the truth, and he told me. He said, "It is because you are black, and if this same business plan was submitted by a white person, the first bank would have approved the loan request." I thanked him for his time and for telling me the truth and proceeded to walk out of his office when he stopped me. He asked if I had been to Automotive Bank on Williams Boulevard, and I said no. I had the bank on my list, but I was under the impression that they only dealt with auto loans, hence their name Automotive Bank.

He told me to sit down while he made a phone call to one of his friends at the bank on the speaker phone. He called a man by the name of Glen Dottollo and told him that he had a man in his office with an excellent business plan and he could not get the loan approved due to racial politics in his bank. Glen then asked him if he would have approved the loan on its merit if there was no such barrier and he said yes. Glen told him to give me his address and send me over to his bank.

When I got to Glen's office, my first impression of him was of a relaxed banker. He dressed casually for a Sr. Vice President of a bank compared to the other bankers I had met. He asked to see my business plan, read it while I was sitting in his office, and asked me a few questions. He looked at me and asked, "When do you plan to start?"

I said, "As soon as I can get a loan."

He asked me to wait, and he went into the next office to speak to his boss, the bank president, and came back within ten minutes. His boss then came in and asked how my day was going. I responded by telling him it would be better if my loan request was approved. He started talking about his recent vacation to the San Francisco Bay area, and how he was relaxed when he was not working.

As he walked back to his office, he said, "Glen, give him what he wants." Just like that, Glen Dottollo approved our loan request. I was then asked to bring a few other documents a day later so they could give me an advance check to start the construction of our Read location. Again, God provided a way for us to move forward with our expansion of Happy Kids.

Now with an advance check on hand, I met with Donald Carriere, the contractor and we went over the approved architectural plan and the time frame for the start and completion of the building. We started digging the foundation for the building about four weeks after our meeting and I shadowed Donald all through the construction of the building.

I used to drive my family to the construction site on Sundays after church. We would get out and walk around viewing the progress and thanking God. One particular Sunday afternoon, we drove up and saw an elderly white couple loading 2x4s and 2x6s wood boards into their truck. It was 1 pm in the afternoon! I asked them what they were doing. The elderly man told me not to worry, the owner had permitted him to take some of the lumber. Deborah and I looked at each other laughing. I turned to him and said, "I never gave you permission to take anything, you are stealing!" That couple unloaded the lumber so fast and burned rubber driving away!

After the building was erected and painted, I installed all the hooks, shelves and other childcare required items needed for us to obtain the final inspections.

About two months before the completion of the building we began hiring and training new staff for the Read location. Also, parents on the waiting list at our Morrison Road location began to pay registration fees for their children in order to secure their place at the new center. We started running advertisements informing the community of our anticipated opening day. The advertising campaign was very successful because on April 3, 1998, the opening day of the center, we had ninety-nine students registered at the center. That was our full licensed capacity. Now operating at full capacity at both locations, my wife and I were very excited about opening our new facility but at the same time we anticipated our workload to be doubled.

Operating both centers was a bit challenging on our management staff. Dealing with the children and parents' issues was not a problem or surprising beyond our expertise however, dealing with an additional twenty employees with different ideas and characters was a challenge, but we made it work by extensive staff training and most important, by adjusting our management style.

Six months after our opening day we started experiencing the same capacity issues since some of the parents at our centers were pregnant and again demanding that a spot should be reserved for their children as soon as they were born and able to attend our infant program. I thought our expansion was fast and wanted to slow it down to give me room to settle from the long planning and construction period.

Once again, everywhere I went, I started seeing more pregnant women as if I were going out there looking for them. I tried to ignore it and then I started having daydreams of a larger center and parents bringing their children to our center and the parking lot filled with cars, but I had no idea what the building looked like or where it was.

Sometimes we get busy with our daily lives and forget the source of our blessings. In my opinion, which is one of the greatest mistakes that we make as humans, we forget that God is still doing miracles in our lives and that He is watching our every move.

We pray and ask for His blessings and when He gives it to us and pour down His blessings upon us, we either are too busy to recognize the opportunities or simply ignore the blessings He places in front of us. We sometimes are too busy to sit still and open our eyes and ears and watch what the spirit of God is saying and showing us.

I gave myself a lot of excuses such as the reluctance

to move forward because of the stress of building a new building, the stress of having to deal with additional employees and the need to slow down our fast rate of expansion. But it all boiled down to the fact that I was becoming comfortable almost to the point of disobedience to God's word and blessings.

But I knew seeing all those pregnant mothers and daydreaming about a larger facility with all the children coming in and out of the building and the parking lot filled with children, that God was speaking to me, and I know what that meant. We needed to build another Happy Kids location bigger than the ones we had. I told my wife that we need to build another building bigger than the current Read Boulevard center and she looked at me as if she had just seen a ghost and inquired how we were going to handle another center in addition to the current two center that we had. My response was that it is going to be okay and that I can see the building completed, parents bringing in their children and the parking lot filled with cars. She said, "I can't see it, but I know you do," and we agreed to pursue the building of another center.

As usual I started driving around looking for land that we could purchase and build a new center. I drove around in the morning, afternoon, evenings, and weekends studying neighborhoods for the flow of foot traffic around existing lands for sale and finally settled on eight pieces of land properties next to each other on Downman and Dwyer Road. It was owned by Dr. Blocker who lived in California and his siblings. Dr. Blocker told me that they had inherited the property from their father and wanted to sell it. The properties had been there for years and were not being used. We made an offer on the properties, and it was accepted, and we moved forward to purchase the properties and further replat it into one large property for us to build on it.

The reaction of our banker at the news of our willingness to build another center was very different this time around and they were willing to provide the financing necessary with very little questions since we have honored our end of the bargain on our previous loans. The funds needed were available and again, I went to Mr. Lewis Clements, and he had to come out of retirement one more time for my sake.

Mr. Clements and I had become friends by working together on our projects. He occasionally called to see how we were doing, and I visited with him at his home on several occasions. When we started discussing what the building will look like, it became clear to me how I had to build the building. I drew the sketch, and he completed the drawing to meet the city code requirement.

After receiving the building permit, we started the construction. For this project, Donald Carriere was not available. I felt confident that I could oversee the project, but I needed a project manager. Through several recommendations, I hired Gladys, a tough and rugged individual. Gladys assisted me in hiring subs to complete the job. One such individual was Willie, the bobcat operator.

During the project, Willie kept giving Gladys a hard time. One day, all of this came to a head at the job site. Willie kept saying that he would punch Gladys out if she were a man. Gladys countered and put her hands up in a boxing stance.

Willie kept saying, "I will knock you out!"

Gladys threw a 1-2 punch and Willie hit the dirt. Needless to say, Willie left Gladys alone after that!

Willie turned out to be very shady. One day on the job, his bobcat broke, and he was unable to continue working. He asked me to rent a bobcat so he could complete the job. I agreed and contacted a local company to rent the bobcat. The company asked if I wanted insurance on the rental. I normally would refuse but my inner voice screamed, "Yes!" So, I added the insurance and set up delivery.

The bobcat was delivered in a few days and Willie was able to get back to work. The same night of the delivery, Willie called me at 10:30pm and said that he was taking an evening drive and passed the jobsite. He noticed the bobcat was not onsite. He asked if I had moved it. I knew nothing about it. Willies replied that it had probably been stolen. I questioned Willie because he lived several miles away and the evening drive seemed suspicious. When I arrived the next day at the jobsite, sure enough, the bobcat was gone. I had to make a police report and file the insurance. Interestingly, Willie disappeared after that.

During this construction, an incident from our initial project came back to irritate us. An acquaintance, who was a contractor, approached me and asked why I had never given him the opportunity to bid on the Read Blvd. job and this construction. I repeated his words, "I only do million-dollar jobs!" He apologized but said he really could use the work. By this time, I had already started the process. It was too late.

What I didn't know was this guy sat on the state contractor's board. The rule stipulated that I needed a licensed contractor to supervise the job. At this juncture, I had not hired one, so I was summoned to Baton Rouge to meet with the board. As he sat on the panel with a smug grin, I was fined one thousand dollars and told to cease construction until I could get a licensed contractor. The guy just knew I was going to run to him to hire him at that very moment. I got up, thanked the panel, and left the office without speaking to him. His face just dropped. I left and that was how I hired Gladys.

Upon completion of the building, we applied for and received our childcare licensing permit with a capacity of one hundred and sixty-three. We had eighty children when we opened the center in May 2000. Within six months, we had one hundred one thirty-five children enrolled. We eventually maxed out our capacity. With our fast-paced expansion, I continued to look for opportunities to purchase lands for our future expansions.

I found a property that was on Carrollton Road by Xavier University that I felt would be a good location for a childcare center. When I contacted the owner of the property, he asked if I was from McDonalds. McDonalds? I thought that was strange. He insisted that he was only going to sell his property to McDonalds because he liked their food and not Burger King. I contacted him again about five more times and he always asked if I was from McDonalds. Each time I said no, but I would like to buy his land and he refused. He adamantly stated he was only going to sell his land to McDonalds. A few years later I drove past the property, behold he had sold the land to McDonalds, and they had built a new McDonalds restaurant on it. I guess he knew the type of business he wanted on his property!

God has been so good to me and my family. He showed us favor and continued to bless us with the work we were doing and for the work we did at Happy Kids in

New Orleans. Our curriculum was not only based on the requirements of the childcare licensing but also based on loving care due to our Christian beliefs. Regarding Mr. Lewis Clements, I persuaded him not to fully retire. He was not only a skilled architect but also a truly remarkable individual.

Some of our first children at Happy Kids!

This was our second Happy Kids location on Read Blvd. New Orleans, Louisiana. We opened in May 1998; completely filled.

Our Downman Road location opened in May 2000. By this time, we had perfected the school design.
It was a beautiful building.

Graduation Day at Happy Kids.
Downman Road, June 2001.

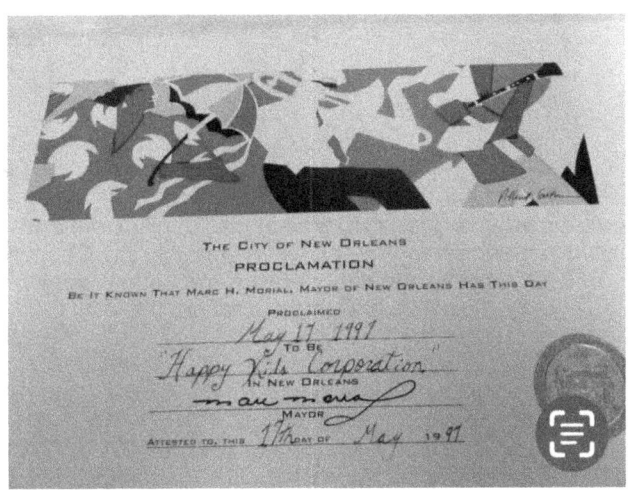

We were recognized by the Mayor's Office in the City of
New Orleans and had a day proclaimed in our honor.
It was a great day and Councilwoman Ellen Hazeur (now Judge)
really supported our efforts.

New Orleans City Council

Proclamation

WHEREAS, the City of New Orleans is renowned for its food, festivals, famous citizens and foreign visitors; and

WHEREAS, the City Council takes great pride in paying tribute to events and activities; now, therefore

BE IT PROCLAIMED BY THE CITY OF NEW ORLEANS that this Council recognizes:

Congratulations
Happy Kids Corporation
On The Occasion of Your
First Annual Family Day
"Parents and Teachers Working Together"

In the name of and by the authority vested in the Council of the City of New Orleans

May 17, 1997

After our first year in business, we held a "Family Day" and received
this proclamation from the New Orleans City Council.
God really showed us favor and poured out
His blessings upon us.

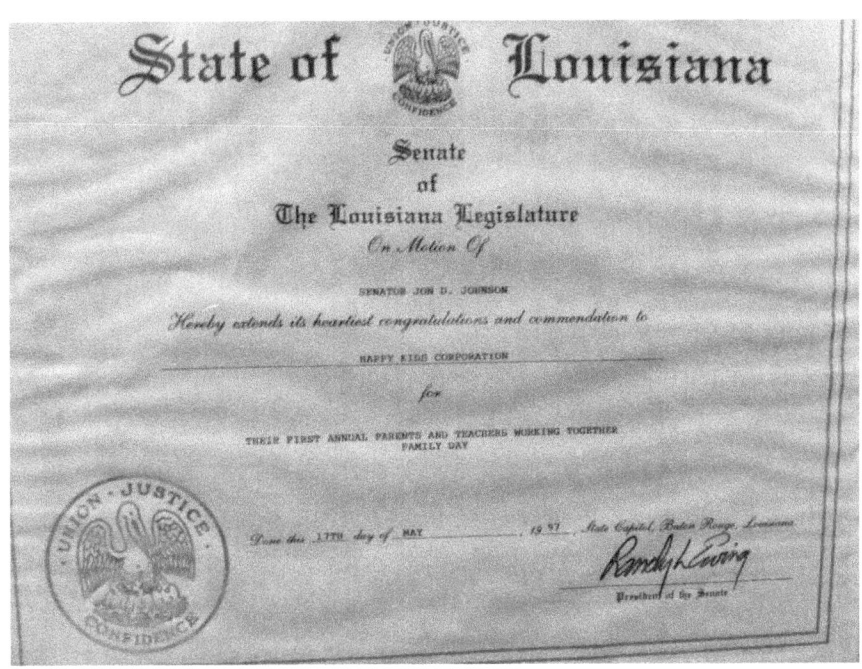

We were also recognized by the Louisiana State Legislature.

The Preschool Class on Downman Road was invited to say the Pledge of Allegiance at the United Way's Women's Leadership Initiative Luncheon on February 14, 2005.

Pictured from the top left: Asst. Teacher Schwanna Johnson, Teacher Diedre Young, Executive Director, Deborah Irabor, Louisiana Governor Kathleen Blanco, and Asst. Director Terry Crosby. Our children were smart, articulate and just a great bunch of kids!

Hurricane Katrina

The drive to escape Hurricane Katrina's wrath; from New Orleans to Houston was one of the most difficult drives of my life. Alone in the car, I felt God's presence in my vehicle, and I knew the Lord was with me but what I did not know was how difficult the journey was going to be and how long it would take.

Back in early 2003 the Lord started speaking to me by asking me a series of questions as to what I would do if there was a storm that destroys the city and destroys our buildings. What would happen to all the employees that depended on us for their livelihood? What would happen to their children? I continued to think about the questions and the more I thought about it the more I realized that I did not have an answer to the questions, meaning I was not prepared for the disaster if it occurred. I did not understand the full ramifications of the question if that happened and what my response should be in regard to all the people that depended on us for their livelihood in preparation for a disaster that may destroy the city. What would happen to me and my family financially if there was a disaster of that magnitude?

I knew that living in New Orleans there was a yearly threat of hurricanes. Evacuating the city for a safer place and then returning after two, three or four days had become a routine of events over the years. My spirit continued to be troubled with these questions. I spoke with my wife about my concerns. We knew we were not prepared for such a calamity. But the question was, how do you prepare for a situation such as the complete destruction of your city? We talked a little about it and prayed that it does not happen then we proceeded to move on to our daily life.

During the summer of 2003, my spirit was troubled again concerning this issue and I told my wife that we needed to expand by building a new facility in the Baton Rouge area. I also had a conversation with our management staff, and they were all saying please stop saying that the city may be destroyed in a coming hurricane. However, I started looking for a suitable place outside of New Orleans but close to Baton Rouge to build a new facility. I was not successful in finding land or a building that agreed with my spirit.

On August 28, 2004, Hurricane Isaac was in the Gulf of Mexico, and we had to evacuate from New Orleans to Houston as New Orleans was in the projected path of the hurricane. We were invited to come and stay with one of our friends (Charlye) from our doctorate program cluster. Charlye lived in Spring, Texas, a suburb northwest of Houston. While staying with Charlye, she mentioned that her brother, Dennis, was a contractor.

When I met Dennis, I asked if he could drive me around so that I could see the cost of land in the area. We spent a few hours driving along Ella Boulevard in the direction of FM 1960 W. I found a property that I was interested in on Ella Boulevard and Romano Business Park. I thought it would be a good location for a new facility in the Houston area, however, the price per square foot was a little out of our price range. I was still interested in the land. I told Dennis I could make it work, and I called to speak with the seller's agent several times. None of my telephone calls were returned. I then asked Dennis to back up and drive on down the street, which he did, but I did not see any land that I was interested in. I also asked him to stop his truck so I could walk around to have a feel for the area. He parked his truck on Rolling Creek Drive, and we walked back to the same land on Ella Boulevard, and I was convinced that was the location of our first facility in Houston. Dennis and I went back to his sister's house.

The next day I drove to Ella Boulevard looking at the land. The more I looked at it the more I wanted it, but the real estate agent listed on the sign would not return my calls

I continued driving around and parked my truck in the same area that Dennis had parked his truck the previous day. I got out of my truck to walk around. As I continued to wonder why the agent listed on the sign for the Ella Boulevard property would not return my calls, I decided to walk towards the land anyway and take another look at it.

When I started walking towards Ella Boulevard land, I heard a voice that said, "turn around." I looked around but saw no one so I continued my walk toward Ella Boulevard from Rolling Creek and Romano Business Park. Upon getting onto the property, I walked around it and towards FM 1960 to observe the foot traffic in the area. Afterward, I walked back to my truck, got in and started to drive towards FM 1960 from Rolling Creek Dr. Again, I heard the voice say, "turn around." I parked my truck, got out, looked around and I walked back to Romano Business Park but saw nothing of interest to me. A few minutes later as I was walking back to my truck, I heard the voice again saying, "turn around." I stopped and turned around and saw a large parcel of land of about two acres. The land was too big for what we needed and there was no sign that it was for sale, so I moved on.

Again, as I started walking back to my truck, after a few steps I heard the voice again, "turn around," but this time the voice was louder as if it was coming from all around me. I turned around and walked back to where I was standing and decided to walk towards the land. About six steps into the property, I stepped on a piece of plywood with stakes on it and decided to pick it up. When I picked it up, it was a for sale sign with the landowner's contact information written on it.

I called the number, and the owner answered. I told him that I was interested in the land. He discussed the prices and I felt it was beyond my reach and asked him if he was willing to divide the land into two plots of land on which he agreed. He asked me what side of the land I would be interested in if he split the land into two as I suggested. I responded that I would prefer the corner lot which would be on Rolling Creek Dr. and Romano Business Park. We continued our conversation as to the asking price and we made a deal over the phone and agreed to meet the next morning. We met and signed our agreement on a piece of paper and later finalized the deal with help from Dennis when we got back to New Orleans. That was how we acquired the land on Rolling Creek Dr.

Upon our return to New Orleans after evacuating to Houston from Hurricane Isaac, the thought of the city being destroyed by a hurricane was constantly on my mind. I talked to my wife and our management team about it again and they did not appreciate my constant conversation of the topic. We all continued business as usual as Hurricane Isaac did not do any major damage to the city as expected. A lot of rain but no major damage due to the shift eastward.

On a different note, on December 25, 2004, Christmas day something happened in New Orleans that I had never experienced. I was sitting in my home office where we lived on Hayne Boulevard looking out of the window and suddenly it started snowing. I thought that I was having a problem with my eyesight hence I opened the front door and walked out, and it was snowing. I went back inside the house and announced to everyone that it was indeed snowing outside. We all went back outside, and the children played in the snow. It was so beautiful. The grounds covered in snow reminded me of my days in graduate school when I was in Baltimore, Maryland.

Now into the summer of 2005, I felt I was a little late in preparing for the construction of the Houston building however, I moved forward by arranging for the financing with our bankers and had Mr. Clements make some changes from our Downman facility construction plans to be used for the Houston building. I contacted Dennis, my Houston contact who is a contractor, so we could move forward to break ground in 2005. We prepared by updating and adjusting our building plans for approval by the Harris County Permit Office, we eventually obtained all the necessary building permits to start construction. I figured expanding our business into Houston would help if New Orleans experienced a catastrophe. Our employees would have a place to work.

In my mind, building more centers in Houston will answer the question that was troubling my spirit. I figured within five years; we should be able to build three centers if business moved in the same pace as we were in New Orleans.

Little did we know that the calm summer of 2005 was the calm before the storm. On August 23, 2005, a tropical depression formed in the Bahamas and became a tropical storm the next day. I can still hear the voice of our cherished meteorologist, Bob Breck, advising the citizens of New Orleans to be prepared to get out of the city that the storm would be a big one and be very bad if it made its way into the Gulf of Mexico. "Get out of the city if it gets in the Gulf!" he said. The storm moved rapidly into the Gulf of Mexico and started to intensify. While the storm was in the Gulf of Mexico, my wife and children were visiting family members in Lumberton, Mississippi.

On Saturday, I called my wife and advised her about the impending storm, and she said they had not heard of the storm and were unaware of any coming storm since they were having a picnic, and everyone was eating fish and enjoying themselves. I advised her to come back home so we could evacuate to Houston.

Upon their arrival home, we watched the storm movement on television while we prepared to evacuate from the city for a few days with the assumption that we would be back as soon as the storm passes. I helped load up the Suburban, our three boys, two dogs (Rocky and Mr. T) and my wife but I stayed behind to wait for the installation of the hurricane shutters for our front door that we had been waiting to get installed for eight months. Of all the days, they called to say they were coming that Saturday.

I then went back upstairs with a beautiful view towards the lake watching as my wife came back upstairs and I could see in her eyes that she was worried. She wanted me to leave for Houston as soon as the installation was completed without delay.

As my family drove off to Houston away from Katrina's path, I felt better that they would not have to fight the late evacuation traffic that would be very heavy in the coming days. After the hurricane shutter installation was completed, I was tired and decided to rest a little on the sofa in the living room so I would have a little energy for the drive to Houston.

When I woke up, I realized that I had slept longer than I thought. I walked outside to the street and everywhere was calm, no sight of car movement. I was shocked that I may have missed my opportunity to get out of the city before the roads were closed because it had begun to rain. I raced back into the house and grabbed my already packed bag and headed for the car to try and get out of New Orleans.

I called my friend Pastor Paul; we had planned to leave the city and evacuate together, and he stated that he was not leaving and planned to stay in his apartment because he did not think it was going to be as bad as forecasted. Against my pleas and advice, he insisted he was staying in his apartment, and he stayed and did not evacuate from the city.

When I got to the I-10 Freeway, via Hayne to Downman Road, to say the road was congested is an understatement. All lanes were opened in the direction of I-10 West. Trying to navigate my way out of New Orleans was challenging. It was raining, traffic was heavy, and the

New Orleans police had begun closing the freeway because it was also windy and dangerous to drive. However, when I got to the Bonnet Carre Spillway past Loyola Drive, the wind picked up and traffic slowed down to a halt. I continued to navigate my way out of New Orleans through Baton Rouge to Lake Charles to finally get to the Texas state line after eighteen hours of driving. On a normal day it takes about six hours to get from New Orleans to Houston.

After a rest stop at the Texas Welcome Center, I continued my journey to Houston to join my family who was staying at a downtown Houston hotel. Upon my arrival, we watched the television most of the night looking for any news about Hurricane Katrina's approach toward the city of New Orleans.

On August 29, 2005, Hurricane Katrina made landfall in south Louisiana after shifting to the east and sparing New Orleans a direct hit. The damage to New Orleans and the surrounding coastal areas of Mississippi and Alabama was extensive. The levies that were meant to protect New Orleans from flood waters were breached and over 1800 people lost their lives and billions of dollars in property damage. All our properties, including our home and three Happy Kids centers were destroyed. Pastor Paul was evacuated by helicopter from his apartment roof top after three days by the United States National Guard.

About ten days after Hurricane Katrina's landfall, my wife and I went to New Orleans to see the extent of the damage caused by the hurricane. It was horrific and the city looked like a war zone. When I saw the damage to our home and preschool buildings, I felt great sadness and could not hold back the tears in my eyes. At that point, I knew that it would be difficult for us to come back and reside in New Orleans.

Returning to Houston my wife and I discussed the future of our family and our future path. We moved ahead with the construction of our first Happy Kids Preschool building on the land we had acquired on Rolling Creek Dr. We had our children enrolled in school and eventually decided to live in the Houston area because it was better for them. The school system and environment were much better and would allow for better growth despite the challenges of forced relocation.

We tried to make the transition as smooth as possible for our children, so we bought a house in Spring and moved from the apartment we were living in. However, my children wanted to go back to New Orleans because they missed their life there and we understood how they felt. In the spring of 2006, we decided to take them to New Orleans for a visit, to see for themselves the state of the city caused by Hurricane Katrina. After our visit to New Orleans, they understood the reason we chose not to go back but to remain in the Houston area.

Now in Houston and all our employees scattered in different places around the country, we worried about how they were doing. I asked my wife to search and call all our employees to make sure that they got out of New Orleans safe and get their current banking information so we could continue to pay them. We would inform them that as soon as we completed and opened the Houston building, they were welcome to relocate to Houston and resume their positions.

While this was taking place, we continued with the construction of our Rolling Creek Dr. building. After the building slab was poured, we were running short of funds to pay the contractors because we were unable to withdraw money for the construction project or locate our banker, Glenn. Glenn worked at Metro bank (formally Automotive Bank) as the vice president for commercial lending and he was our banker for the construction project. He had also left New Orleans to seek safety from Hurricane Katrina with his family and all the banks were flooded and the financial institutions were in disarray.

At that time the bank did not have any locations outside of the New Orleans metropolitan area. I spoke with Dennis, the contractor that was helping with the construction of our building, and explained the situation and urged them to continue working. As soon as I heard from our banker, I would pay him and all the workers.

He agreed and we moved forward with the building project. About two weeks after the discussion with Dennis, Glenn called and said that he had been thinking about me and knew that I would need money to pay the workers. He asked if I could meet him in Baton Rouge to pick up a check. I gladly accepted and went to Baton Rouge the next day to pick up the check. I paid the contactors and workers. Eventually, we completed the building construction, applied for licensing, and opened our Happy Kids Preschool Rolling Creek Center. As an added bonus, we hired our New Orleans employees that wanted a job.

This is our home on Hayne Blvd. before Hurricane Katrina.
We moved here in November 2001.
I designed and directed the building of this house myself.

This is an aerial view of our home on Hayne Blvd taken
August 2005 after Hurricane Katrina ravaged New Orleans.

Happy Kids Preschool on Rolling Creek, Houston, Texas.
We opened in May 2006.

Picking Up The Pieces

In the aftermath of Hurricane Katrina, New Orleans East bore the brunt of nature's fury, leaving the community in ruins and shattering the dreams of its youngest residents. Among the casualties were the two Happy Kids Preschools, cherished institutions of early education that had nurtured countless children over the years. However, as the storm clouds receded, our indomitable spirit rallied to rebuild, even in the face of formidable challenges.

The initial struggle began with navigating the labyrinth of governmental entities. Red tape and bureaucratic hurdles seemed insurmountable as our Happy Kids team sought permits and approvals for the reconstruction. The roadblocks were numerous, but with unwavering determination, we persevered. The desire to give the children of New Orleans East a safe and nurturing environment was an unwavering source of motivation.

Then there was the issue of insurance, a matter that had homeowners and businesses alike wringing their hands. We were no exception. Receiving fair settlements was an uphill battle, with insurance adjusters seemingly minimizing the extent of the damage. Deborah and I were put to the test, but we were determined to see our preschools rise again.

One of the most heart-wrenching challenges was the lack of people returning to the area. Many families had been displaced, scattering to different parts of the country, making it difficult for Happy Kids to anticipate the number of students who would return. With the future uncertain, we needed to make decisions based on hope rather than certainty.

United Way of Greater New Orleans, more specifically, Todd Battiste and Jocelyn Jenkins emerged as vital partners during this trying time. Todd was the Vice President of Children and Families and Jocelyn was his assistant. Their support and resources proved invaluable, helping Happy Kids navigate the complex process of rebuilding and ensuring that we had access to the necessary tools to bring our vision to life. United Way's commitment to the community was a beacon of hope for the Happy Kids team, and their collaboration breathed life into the reconstruction effort. To this day, I consider Todd a brother.

I spent many months overseeing the construction on Downman Road. I made countless trips from Houston to New Orleans. Racking up hotel bills and sometimes having to sleep in my Chevrolet Suburban truck for lack of available hotel room. It was difficult because getting workers was so difficult. When I found contractors, many were not honest.

I had hired a Dominican contractor who brought in a crew. When I came in, I noticed the workers looking at me really funny, sometimes with contempt. On one occasion, Deborah came with me on a trip. As I was speaking with the contractor on the outside, Deborah went inside the building looking around. After about ten minutes, Deborah came outside and asked to speak to me in private. Deborah began to tell me what happened when she went inside. Deborah spoke Spanish. She said she saw a lady in one of the rooms cooking. There was a small toddler playing around. She said she went in and began playing with the baby. When she spoke to the woman in Spanish, the woman began to say that her husband and the other workers had not been paid since they had started the job. They had been on the job for several weeks. Deborah told her that I paid the boss or "jefe" each Friday. The lady shook her head and said the boss said that I refused to pay but they needed to keep working.

When I heard this story, the woman and the workers began to come outside and circle the Contractor. I confronted him with Deborah's story and at first, he tried to deny it but he finally had to admit it in front of the workers that he had indeed been paid.

His excuse was he had to pay for the food and the rooms, and he was deducting it from their pay. The workers started getting angry and saying things I did not understand but I knew they were threats. The contractor began begging me to help him because they wanted to cut him with a knife. I begged the workers not to harm him. I had to pay the workers the balance of what I owed the contractor to get them to stand down. Deborah and I got into the car and got out of there. I had to find a new crew after that!

I had another incident with a gentleman who was putting on the doors in the center. He really didn't know what he was doing. He made a lot of claims but in the end his workmanship was horrible. I asked him to leave. He refused and began jumping up and down, kicking in the doors and hitting them with a hammer! But I was ready for him with my big stick and machete I kept in my Suburban truck.

So many times, I had to do the work myself. It was on this job that I severely injured my back when I fell off a platform hanging sheetrock. This incident began a longtime issue with back pain which I eventually had to have surgery three times to correct.

One remarkable moment in the journey was the arrival of Kaboom, an organization dedicated to creating safe and exciting play spaces for children. They came forward with a generous donation to build a brand-new playground for our Happy Kids Preschool on Downman Road. Kaboom partnered with State Farm Insurance to make the playground a reality.

During the 2006 Bayou Classic, over 150 volunteers showed up to help build the playground. The delight on every face while constructing our new playground was truly captivating. It symbolized resilience and showcased the community's unity in providing a brighter future for the children.

The months of hard work, dedication, and countless setbacks finally culminated in a triumphant day on May 1, 2007. The Happy Kids Preschool on Downman Road was ready to welcome children once again. The laughter of children filled the air, echoing through the newly reconstructed classrooms, and the heartwarming sight of parents dropping off their little ones was a testament to our resilience.

As we reopened, Deborah and I made a difficult decision to sell the Read Blvd. Center. It was a tough choice, but one made with the children's best interests in mind. Consolidating our resources allowed us to focus on the Downman Road location, ensuring that we could provide the best possible environment for our students and continue our mission of nurturing young minds.

Rebuilding Happy Kids Preschool in New Orleans East was a labor of love, a story of unwavering dedication to the community's children. Through adversity, bureaucratic hurdles, and financial struggles, our commitment never wavered. The support of organizations like United Way and the generosity of Kaboom brought a ray of hope to our journey.

Unfortunately, in February 2017, a tornado came eastward down Downman Road. It hit the building and set off a chain of events that led to the fire which burned down the building. We made the decision not to rebuild because we believed that it was time for us to move on.

This was our Downman Center after Hurricane Katrina. The water was over 8 feet in the building and when the water receded, a major exit point was through Deborah's office window. The amount of trash was overwhelming. However, we made it through.

We came back better and stronger on Downman Road. We re-opened in May 2007. Our logo was designed by the brother of one of our students.

The Kaboom Playground built with State Farm.
Many children enjoyed this playground!

Deborah and I attended Todd's wedding to Carin in Montego Bay, Jamaica. Also pictured is Jocelyn Jenkins (back right).

The Vision of MI 3 Center

MI 3 Center is a place built with hope, faith, and lots of love, where the goodness of God can be felt and seen. As an ordained minister of the Gospel of Christ, it is my belief that preaching on a church pulpit is not the only way to spread the gospel. Our lives should minister to others so they can see the goodness of God in us even though we are imperfect.

Using sports as a means to spread the gospel and to have an impact in the lives of both the old and young in our community, I felt the calling of God to build a place where people could come in and feel safe while participating in the sport of their choice whether it be basketball or volleyball.

To say that God works in mysterious ways is an understatement. This is how MI 3 Center came into existence. In 2009, my son Michael was playing AAU basketball and some of the games were played at League American Sports Center off the 610W Beltway just passed West Road. I had to drive our family to the games.

On one occasion as I was sitting in my home office waiting for everyone to be ready, my son, Daniel walked into my office and said he was ready. I then remarked that I did not understand why there were no places closer to the house where they could hold the basketball games. I started complaining that the distance to League America was too far. Daniel then asked, "Why don't you build one?" I replied that it costs a lot of money to build a sports facility. He looked at me and walked out of my home office. I guessed that's what I get for complaining. A few minutes later everyone was ready and off we went to Michael's game.

Over the next several weeks as we were preparing to go to Michael's game at League America, I again started complaining about the driving distance but this time to myself. However, Daniel's words were in my head, "why don't you build one?" I thought building a sports facility was way too expensive and out of my league to go alone. I decided it was not something that I would like to do. Moreover, we were in the childcare business, and I was thinking of building a second Happy Kids Preschool location here in Houston.

While I was driving around looking for a second location where we could build a new Happy Kids facility, God gave me an idea: to build the childcare facility that would include a place where children can come play sports. I had no idea what was playing out in my spirit, but I remained in prayers since I had no clue what a facility like that would look like.

Later that week on a Saturday I went to Happy Kids building to do some maintenance work. After finishing my work, I decided to drive down Ella Blvd. While driving down Ella Blvd, I saw some young kids playing basketball on the grounds of Westfield High School at the outdoor courts. I continued driving past Richey Rd and turned around to go back home. On my way back, I noticed the Spring ISD police officers chasing the young kids who were playing basketball off the Westfield High School grounds. I felt bad for the kids as they were just having fun.

The following Saturday I decided to drive past Westfield High to see if the kids were playing basketball. I did not see a single kid, but I saw at least four Spring ISD police cars, so I assumed that they had been run away again. I thought nothing about it and went home.

A few nights later, I woke up at about 3:00 am in the morning thinking about the young kids at Westfield playing basketball and my previous conversation with Daniel. It played like an unstoppable record in my head. I reached for a pen and a legal pad in my home office and started drawing what a building with a childcare facility and a place to play basketball would look like. I must have drawn the sketch of what the building would be like more than twenty times. I did not like what I drew. Since I could not sleep, I sat in my office until daybreak thinking.

The next night, I decided to work on the sketch backward. I decided to draw a sketch of the basketball courts first and then place a school around it. After several sketches it began to make sense to me, but I still could not make it work the way I wanted it. I could not see the building at its completion in my spirit as I was able to see our Happy Kids buildings during the design process. So, I let the idea go and concentrated on looking for land to build a new Happy Kids building.

A few months later, I was unable to get a good night's sleep. I woke up about 2:00 am and went into my home office and sat in the chair thinking and behold, the Lord let me see the building at its completion. I grabbed a pencil and a legal paper and started sketching the floor plan for the basketball courts with the childcare center on its side, the weight room, offices, and rooms upstairs.

After sketching the building, I started thinking about what it would cost to make it a reality. So, I created a cost analysis on the sketch calling vendors for prices and material costs. I must say that after I received the major project cost, I panicked and decided to opt for four basketball courts instead of eight basketball courts as I originally planned.

One day while I was in my office reworking the floor plan, Daniel came in and asked me what I was doing. I showed him the layout of the planned project and we started talking about it. I mentioned that I couldn't really afford it and I was reducing the courts from eight to four. He suggested for me to make it six courts since there were no other facilities near us with six courts. I then adjusted the plans to six courts. I also received suggestions from Mark Jr. and Michael during this process as well.

I felt good about the finished sketch so I called Dennis Ivy and asked him to design an architectural drawing that would meet the city building code and be approved for construction. It took Dennis about two months to complete and deliver the architectural plans. After receiving the completed plans, I visited my mechanical and electrical engineers in New Orleans to complete their drawing portion of the project. After my New Orleans trip, I contacted a civil and structural engineer in Houston, who developed the civil, structural and foundation design of the project. When all the plans were completed, I asked the engineers for their help on the project projected cost.

Upon evaluating the project plans, I received an estimate indicating that the construction of the building would exceed $5.2 million. The realization of a cost exceeding five million dollars, excluding the expense of acquiring the land, instilled a sense of panic in me.

Amid the economic downturn in the United States in 2009-2011, marked by sluggish job growth and elevated unemployment rates, banks exhibited reluctance to extend substantial loans. Faced with this financial landscape and the anticipated expenses, I made the decision to abandon the plans. Consequently, I folded them and stored them atop my home office cabinet.

My placing the plans away did not stop me from thinking about the project. I could tell my spirit was not happy with me since I was also not happy with my decision to shelf the plans. But the Lord was constantly reminding me in different ways that I needed to build the building.

In May 2011, my wife and I went to Hawaii to attend the World Forum Foundation on childcare and the project was constantly on my mind. While we were in the hotel, my wife, Deborah, asked me to explain the project to her again and I did. She reminded me that since I believed that the Lord wanted me to build the building, I would not be happy until the building was built. I remember saying that for a large building of that size we would need at least five acres of land and it would cost us a lot of money.

That was when I realized that I had been too comfortable where we were, and I was not listening to my inner self. I decided to get on my computer and do a land search in the Northwest Houston area. I found several properties for sale, but one caught my eye, it was approximately fifteen acres of land – way more than we needed for the project.

When we returned to Houston, we drove towards the property address looking for the property and eventually found the land. The address was across the street from Westfield High School, where I saw the young kids playing basketball. On meeting with the landowner, we negotiated and decided to buy the property. We had been attempting to acquire financing for the entire project, but the process was moving so slowly. We realized that the land deal might fall through, so we decided to go ahead and purchase the land cash. Since no financing was involved, the purchase process was fast. With the purchase of the land, I moved forward to trying to secure financing for the project.

After several failed attempts to get financing for the project, I was finally able to persuade the president of a local Houston bank to finance the project for us. However, a few weeks before the closing of the loan, the bank president called me and wanted to go over the numbers again. During our meeting in his office, he suggested that I use the services of his brother who was a contractor. I explained to him that I have my own contractor and thanked him for his offer. He then insisted that the only way he would be comfortable with the project was for his brother to be the general contractor. I refused and he backed out of the deal. I again thanked him for his time and moved on.

During this period, the United States was in a post-recession phase, with the economy remaining sluggish. Banks, particularly unenthusiastic about sizeable construction loan financing deals, were not favoring small business owners. Faced with these economic challenges, I once again put the project on hold. However, in late May 2012, a sense of concern resurfaced within me about moving forward with the project. Despite my willingness, the reluctance persisted due to the financial roadblock in obtaining necessary financing. Also, earlier in April 2012, my prayers regarding both the project and my aspiration to retire intensified. Consequently, I initiated an exit plan from work, aiming to retire in a few years.

In the meantime, I was in conversation with a Christian minister concerning Ordination and he instructed me to go to New Orleans, and visit with one Pastor Benjamin Andrew, who I had never met, and fellowship with him. I called Pastor Andrew and he agreed to meet with me in New Orleans at the Baptist Theological Seminary campus on Gentilly Road in New Orleans.

On May 17, 2012, my wife and I went to New Orleans as planned where we met with Pastor Andrews and one of his friends, Pastor Christopher Allen Moore of the Prayer Tower Church of God in Christ on Willow Street in New Orleans.

As we introduced ourselves Pastor Moore said to me that the Lord asked him to lay hands on me and pray for me. As he laid his hands on me and started praying, he said the Lord spoke to him to tell me that the idea he put in my heart, it is time to build it. I was shocked; this was the first time my wife and I were meeting Pastor Andrew and Pastor Moore.

Further, we had never discussed the project with them. Pastor Moore continued in prayer saying that the plans that I have on the top of my cabinet collecting dust need to be dusted off and built. He further stated that the Lord wanted me to know that the money I needed for the project had been released in Heaven and if I believe it, I will receive it on earth. He stated that the Lord said the time to build is now and when the building is completed as a result, a lot of people will be saved, young children will be saved, and the old will find love again. He continued in his prayers, while laying hands on me and ordained me a Minister of the Gospel of Christ.

After our meeting with Pastors Andrew and Moore, as we were walking back towards our car, I asked my wife, "Why did you tell him about the project?"

Her response was, "I never met them before in my life."

At that moment, we knew the building must be built. When we arrived back home, I updated the business plan for the project, and I continued seeking financing for the project.

We eventually approached and got Gulf Coast Bank & Trust in New Orleans to finance the construction project and MI 3 Center was built. We decided to call the facility MI 3 Center to signify "Mark Irabor" and his three sons. We updated the construction plans, making some changes and applied for building permits.

On May 30, 2013, we started construction of MI 3 Center and completed the construction in July 2014, and we opened our doors officially September 1, 2014.

Here I am, overseeing the formation of the slab. We made sure we prayed and thanked God at each phase of the construction.

It is always great, and my heart is full of joy when I see young men and women playing basketball, or volleyball or just being a spectator, watching others enjoying themselves. MI 3 Center has been involved in our community and spreading love overseas conducting medical and educational missions, helping those that need a little assistance along the way. God was always in the center of the plan all along and He is still doing miracles every day.

Pastor Christopher Moore and Pastor Benjamin Andrews ordained me
in New Orleans on May 17, 2012.
Pastor Moore laid hands on me and prophesized that God told him to
tell me that it's time to build.
This ignited my fire to move forward with my plans
to build MI 3 Center.

Our motto is Faith. Hope. Love. "And abide Faith, Hope, Love, these
three; but the greatest of these is love." 1 Corinthians 13:13

The Academy Side

Wanderlust Chronicles: Embracing the Love of Travel

Blessed by the opportunity to explore some of the most exquisite and captivating places on Earth, I often find myself marveling at the wonders of God's creation. My journey began in Africa, where I grew up, but my first voyage outside the continent took me to the enchanting city of Amsterdam, the capital of the Netherlands, which continues to hold a special place in my heart. This was just the beginning of my adventures, and I yearned to see more of the world's treasures.

Western Europe welcomed me with open arms, and each country I visited had its own unique charm. Venice, a city in Italy perched in the lagoon of the Adriatic Sea, left me in awe of its romantic canals and graceful architecture. The charm of Tuscany, in Italy with its food and beautiful landscape. Beautiful Monte Carlo, in Monaco situated along the French Riviera and the Mediterranean sea with its fascinating museums. The vibrant city of Nice in France, with its azure waters and picturesque streets, lured me into its embrace. Paris, the City of Lights, dazzled me with its history and monumental landmarks like the Eiffel Tower and Louvre Museum. London, England with its rich history dating back to Roman times, offered a glimpse into the past that was simply enthralling. I enjoyed Scotland, with its rich history, winding roads and hills that told the story of its rich history. I cannot forget

Ireland, where I visited family. The beautiful green landscapes, views from the Atlantic Ocean, smell of bourbon and tranquil atmosphere.

Yet, while Western Europe was a magnificent experience, my heart yearned for a different kind of beauty. It led me to the Caribbean nations, where I discovered a cultural resemblance to my African roots. Belize, the Cayman Islands, the Dominican Republic, Jamaica, Virgin Islands, and the Bahamas beckoned with their vibrant music, dance, and traditions. These places not only captivated my senses but also resonated with my soul. The pristine white sand beaches of Aruba left me breathless, and I couldn't help but marvel at the sheer brilliance of nature's design.

My trip to Dubai on the other side of the world, with its modern skyscrapers that touch the clouds and opulent resorts nestled in the desert, left us spellbound by its sheer extravagance. The spice-scented air of the historic Deira district and the vibrant colors of the souks filled with gold, textiles, and fragrant spices transported us to another world.

However, my heart aches to witness the holy cities of Bethlehem and Jerusalem. The thought of treading the same paths as Jesus Christ, the prophets, kings, and sages of old fills me with a profound sense of reverence. The Western Wall, the Church of the Holy Sepulcher, and the Dome of the Rock stand as monuments to faith, history, and the enduring human spirit. To set foot in these sacred places would be a pilgrimage of the soul, a journey that transcends mere tourism.

In my quest to explore the beauty of God's creation, I've come to realize that each corner of the world has its unique story to tell. Whether it's the artistic masterpieces of Europe, the cultural tapestry of the Caribbean or the spiritual sanctuaries of the Middle East, there is a never-ending tapestry of experiences awaiting me.

My journeys around the world have been made even

more memorable by the wonderful company of some great friends. Sunny, with his radiant personality and infectious laughter and JoAnn's keen sense of humor have added a delightful spark to our travels. Charles and Mary have made every trip and cruise we've taken so interesting and fun. Simon and Anna, with their adventurous spirit, have led us off the beaten path to discover the secret wonders in Canada.

And, of course, there's my life's partner, Deborah Joy, who has been my steadfast companion through it all. Our shared experiences, from strolling hand in hand along the canals of Rome to savoring exotic flavors in distant lands, have deepened our love and strengthened our bond. Deborah's presence has been a source of comfort, joy, and love throughout our travels, and I'm grateful for every moment we've shared together.

My dear friends have not only made my journeys more enjoyable but have also brought their unique perspectives and passions to every place we've explored. Together, we've laughed, learned, and created lasting memories that will forever be etched in our hearts.

As I reflect on the places I've been blessed to see and those I yearn to visit, I am filled with gratitude for the opportunity to witness the world's incredible diversity. I hope to continue my journey, discovering the beauty, wonders, and intricacies of each new destination. With an open heart and an adventurous spirit, I will continue to explore, learn, and embrace the magnificence of this world.

Our family in New Orleans...
we're always enjoy cheering on the New Orleans Saints!
Who Dat! January 5, 2020.

Deborah and I in the desert of Dubai, May 2023.

I loved the tranquility and the island vibes of Aruba, June 2022.

Edinburg, Scotland was cold, but we loved it!
September 2022.

We enjoyed the Atlantis in the Bahamas.
Family trip in July 2022.

We always have fun with our friends.
Carnival Cruise, Costa Maya, México May 2022.

Reflections On My Life

As I reflect on my life, I consider my family to be my greatest accomplishment. My journey began when I arrived in the United States as a young man, full of dreams and aspirations. I had come here in search of a good education and an opportunity to better myself and little did I know that this quest would lead me to some of the most precious treasures in my life.

During my pursuit of knowledge, I found not only an education but also a best friend who would become an integral part of my life. We supported each other through thick and thin, and I'm eternally grateful for the unwavering companionship that has enriched my existence.

However, the most remarkable outcome of my journey was the discovery of true love. I met a remarkable woman who shared my dreams and my values. She became my wife and together, we embarked on the beautiful adventure of life. We faced challenges and celebrated triumphs side by side, and through it all, our love grew stronger.

The real bonus in my life, though, is the family we built together. We were blessed with three incredible children who brought boundless joy and purpose into our lives. Watching them grow, learn, and develop their unique personalities has been a source of immeasurable pride and fulfillment. These three children are the living embodiment of my dreams and hopes, and I consider them my greatest accomplishments.

As time passed, our family continued to expand, and

we were graced with the arrival of three grandchildren (so far)! The joy of being a grandparent is beyond words, and it has added a new layer of happiness and love to our family. Each grandchild is a little bundle of joy; a reminder of the circle of life, and a source of endless laughter and love.

To complete the picture, my daughters-in-law joined our family, bringing their unique qualities and strengths. Their presence has added depth to our family dynamics, and I'm grateful for the beautiful connections we've formed.

When I look back on my life, I can honestly say that nothing beats the fulfillment I've found in my family. They are the reason for my happiness, my motivation, and my greatest source of pride. The bonds we share are unbreakable, and I cherish every moment we spend together.

As for regrets, I can honestly say that I have none. I believe that God has been good and faithful to me, guiding my path and allowing me to make the choices that led me to this beautiful family.

I see myself as a work in progress, continually learning, growing, and striving to be the best version of myself. With the love and support of my family, I have no room for regret, only gratitude for the blessings that have filled my life.

In the end, it's the love, laughter, and unity within my family that make every day a gift, and I consider them my greatest accomplishment, a treasure that I will forever hold dear in my heart.

Grandchildren add a wonderful perspective to your life.
I feel so blessed!

Blessed.

My youngest son, Michael, at one of his birthday celebrations.

Daniel and Amanda were married April 23, 2022.

Danisha and Mark were married July 22, 2023.

Wisdom of My Father

In this journey of life, certain decisions stand out with remarkable clarity, weaving a narrative that shapes our identity and influences the choices we make. For me, one of these defining threads is the sage advice bestowed upon me by my father during my formative years. As a young man poised at the crossroads of possibilities, his counsel echoed with unwavering conviction: "Get a good education."

This seemingly straightforward advice carried profound implications, rooted in my father's personal journey and the aspirations he harbored for me. Born into a family of farmers, my father experienced firsthand the toil and hardship of a farmer's life. His parents, resilient and industrious as they were, eked out a meager existence from the land. Yet, my father, fueled by a relentless desire for a better life, made a pivotal decision that would chart the course of his destiny — he left the village for the bustling city of Lagos.

Lagos, with its promises of opportunity and prosperity, became the crucible in which my father's character was forged. However, the initial days in the city proved arduous. The complexity of urban life, coupled with the challenges of navigating an unfamiliar terrain, tested his resolve. Yet, in the midst of adversity, he found the need to seek not only survival but a profound transformation through education.

With a tenacity born out of necessity, my father enrolled in correspondence courses. As he toiled in the day to make ends meet, he devoted his nights to learning, poring over correspondence materials. This dual life of labor and learning became the crucial factor in which he refined his intellect and expanded his horizons.

His journey mirrored the classic tale of self-improvement, where education served as the catalyst for upward mobility. The knowledge he acquired through those correspondence courses became the currency with which he could navigate the intricate pathways of life in the city. The notion that education was not merely a means to an end, but a lifelong companion on the journey of self-discovery, became ingrained in his philosophy.

The importance of education, as relayed by my father, was not confined to the realm of securing a job or achieving financial stability, although these were undeniable facets. Education, he asserted, was the key to unlocking doors that remained closed to those without the tools of knowledge.

As I absorbed these lessons, I found myself on a parallel trajectory of academic pursuits. In echoing my father's footsteps, I, too, pursued a higher education, recognizing its potential to reshape my destiny. The corridors of university became the crucible where theories were tested, perspectives were broadened, and the foundation for a future of possibilities was laid. The resonance of my father's advice was palpable as I delved into the diverse realms of knowledge, cognizant that each lesson was a steppingstone toward a future defined by the transformative power of education.

The impact of education on my father's life was evident in the opportunities that unfolded before him. From the dusty fields of the village to the bustling streets of Lagos, he was able to enlist into the Nigerian Police Force, progressed and retired as a commissioner.

Yet, my father's counsel extended beyond the realms of personal success. He envisioned education as a force that could catalyze societal change. Having witnessed the disparity between the opportunities available to those with and without education, he became an advocate for the democratization of knowledge. He believed that an educated populace was the cornerstone of a progressive society, and he imparted this belief to me as a legacy to be upheld.

As I reflect on my own educational odyssey, I recognize the echoes of my father's journey. The challenges may have evolved, the landscape of opportunities may have shifted, but the essence remains unchanged — the conviction that education is the cornerstone of personal and societal progress. This belief, passed down from father to son, is a legacy that transcends generations, a torchbearer lighting the path for those who follow.

The resonance of my father's advice reverberates in every academic milestone I achieved, in every lesson learned, and in every challenge overcome. It echoes in the choices made, the sacrifices endured, and the unwavering commitment to continuous learning. It is a reminder that education is not a finite destination but an ongoing journey—a journey that shapes character, hones intellect, and fosters a sense of responsibility to contribute meaningfully to the world.

The significance of education in the context of family life

also became apparent as I assumed the role of a provider. The stability and security afforded by a good education translated into a solid foundation for my family. It became the bedrock upon which aspirations were built, dreams were nurtured, and a sense of continuity was established. In this, I witnessed firsthand the ripple effect of my father's foresight—a legacy that transcended personal success to encompass the well-being of those entrusted to my care.

The best advice my father gave me as a young man transcends the realm of conventional wisdom. It is a profound testament to the transformative power of education—a power that reshapes destinies, breaks the shackles of circumstance, and paves the way for a future defined by limitless possibilities. As I carry forward this legacy, I do so with a deep appreciation for the wisdom embedded in those simple yet profound words: "Get a good education."

My Dad was able to see me receive my Doctorate Degree in May 2005. It was a great day. Also in this picture is Deborah's Dad, Al Ford.

Lessons For My Sons

My one wish for my children that I have learned from my life's lessons is for them to put God first in their lives. Anything you want to do or achieve in life; you should present it to God first and must put God first.

The Bible says in Proverbs 3: 5-6: "*Trust in the Lord with all your heart and lean not on your own understanding. In all your ways acknowledge Him, and He will direct your path.*"(NKJV)

When they put God first in their lives, God will do amazing things in their lives beyond their comprehension. God has been good to me and has blessed me and I want them to remember the goodness of God and praise Him for it. They must remember that it is God that sustain us through life because of His faithfulness.

They must not take for granted God's goodness. Do not forget to thank and praise God for His goodness. I pray they pass that on to my grandchildren, great-grandchildren, and the generation beyond. Also, I want them to know God for themselves.

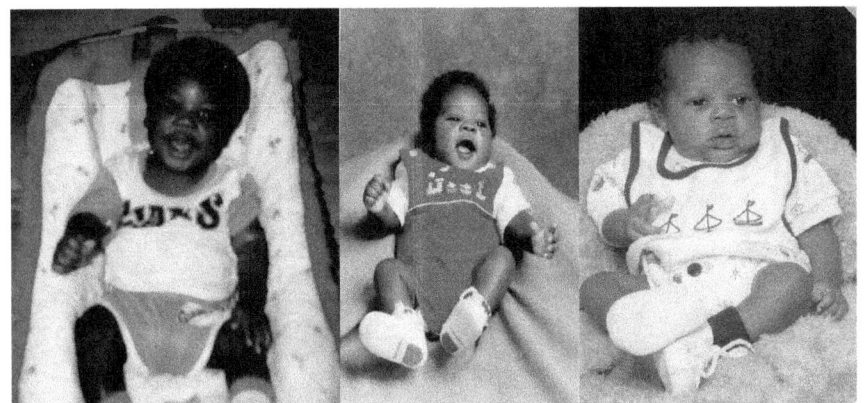

Mark Jr.   **Daniel**   **Michael**

The Struggle Within

"It is of the Lord's mercies that we are not consumed because His compassions fail not. They are new every morning: great is thy faithfulness." Lamentations 3:22-23 (KJV)

As a child I have always believed in God and His majestic power. I also believe in our Lord Jesus Christ as my personal Lord and Savior. Sometimes I doubt my own abilities to carry forward and achieve a set goal, but I have never doubted my faith in God. I know that God created everything for His own purpose, and He allows us to enjoy what He has created. Any time I have faced doubt, I always placed the blame on myself for either not being still enough to listen or open my eyes to see beyond what is in front of me.

Even though I know that I have some flaws and I am not perfect, I try to work diligently to make sure that my actions are aligned with my faith. As a human being, I have sometimes failed in that endeavor, but I am a work in progress toward that perfection that is only found in Christ.

I was about twelve years old when I got saved and believed that God's hand has been upon my life in everything that I lay my hands on to do even in my deepest failures.

I thank God for His mercies and grace.

A Picture is Worth a Thousand Words

It is impossible to include all the pictures that have represented my life, but I have included a few that I enjoy.

In my younger days in Nigeria. I left a very young man, full of dreams and ambition.

I have always loved the Atlantis Hotel in the Bahamas.

Our beautiful family celebrating Mark and Danisha's wedding, July 2023. It was a beautiful day.

I celebrated my birthday in Aruba on a Party Bus! We had an exciting time. Aruba is a place you can't just visit once!

My Dad had the opportunity to come and see my business thriving in person. He was extremely proud of Deborah and I

Our family celebrating the nuptials of Daniel and Amanda, April 2022.
Michael is the last one to take the plunge! We are waiting!

Who knew? We were born 12 days apart, but on different sides
of the world. It was destined that we would meet.

My beautiful bride and I. She looks just like she did in 1982!

Changing Faces,
Unchanging Essence

Honestly, I feel I am the same person. The major difference is that I am older, more mature and a little wiser now than when I was as an adolescent. As a child, I had the constant need of being accepted and fitting into the "group" because we moved around a lot due to my father's job as a police officer. We lived in so many different cities which made it difficult to make long lasting friendships with my peers. As a teenager, having attended boarding schools (St. Joseph's and St. Patrick's), I felt more confident in myself and in my ability to define my goals. I was quiet, focused, significant risk taker, and wanted to see the world for all it had to offer.

I held the view that I must have a good foundation in my beliefs, get a good education, and work extremely hard in high school while balancing my interests in tennis and soccer. When I was twelve years old, I got saved and accepted Jesus Christ as my Lord and Savior and tried to do the right thing in keeping with the Christian faith. In addition, I also kept with our tradition of trusting and honoring one's word, helping others, and respecting my elders.

When I was eighteen years old, I was charting my

own course in the direction that I believed God was leading me and becoming more settled in the person that I am today. As an adult, I am still a very quiet person in my ways. Maybe the right word is very reserved; still focused but taking less risk in life. I still believe that getting a good education with hard work helps in facilitating a successful life. But I must admit that more than often I question the idea or definition of being successful. I sometimes ask what will I tell my younger self? I guess I will advise my younger self to have fun and worry less.

But one thing I do know is that my path in life has been designed by God. It is through my faith in God that He has allowed me to enjoy His blessings in this journey called life.

This picture was taken at St. Joseph's College in Otuo. I enjoyed sports like soccer and tennis.

Life's reflections

Gratitude in Words: A Heartfelt Thank You

"Rejoice always, pray continually, give thanks in all circumstances; for this is God's will for you in Christ Jesus"

1 Thessalonians 5:16-18

First, I thank God for His love, blessings, and faithfulness towards me and my family. Looking back at my life I can see the hand of God on how in His majestic ways and grand masterplan worked things out in my favor. Even for the things that I could not see or perceive I know He was there, and He is still doing great things in my life.

I would like to thank my parents for instilling the value of education, hard work, and discipline in me.

I would like to thank my high school classmate that gave me one of his Dillard University's admission packages. It's unfortunate that I cannot remember his name. Mr. Igueze, the accountant and one of my father's tenants, gave me the bank drafts that made it possible for me to pay Dillard University's admissions application fee. A big thank you to Kenneth Iduwonyi for allowing me to shadow him and teaching me the steps necessary to navigate the process necessary in obtaining my travel documents.

I want to thank my children, grandchildren and especially my lovely wife, Deborah, for their support and love as we continue to grow together and make great memories in this journey called life.

There are a lot of other people that have crossed my path along the way and helped me in one way or another and I am grateful. I pray that God bless them for the assistance they have rendered to me, and I hope that life has treated them well. I am truly blessed, and I thank you all. Much Love!

"Trust in the Lord with all thine heart; and lean not unto thine own understanding.

In all thy ways acknowledge Him, and He shall direct thy paths."

Proverbs 3:5-6 (KJV)

www.ingramcontent.com/pod-product-compliance
Lightning Source LLC
Chambersburg PA
CBHW071144130626
46553CB00004B/1509